PRAISE FOR MARK BROWN

HYROX Playbook breaks a complex event into a scalable, step-by-step plan—perfect for busy athletes who want real results without guesswork. The practical guidance on programming and race-day strategies makes it an indispensable reference for anyone serious about HYROX.

DR. ELENA KOVÁCS, SENIOR EXERCISE
PHYSIOLOGIST, HORIZON INSTITUTE

The book demystifies HYROX's unique format with precise movement breakdowns, proven pacing templates, and sensible recovery protocols that translate into tangible gains.

MARCUS REED, HEAD COACH, VELOCITY
PERFORMANCE TRAINING

A thoughtful fusion of science and pragmatism, HYROX Playbook gives readers a clear roadmap—from foundation workouts to race-day tactics—so HYROX becomes a catalyst for lifelong fitness.

DR. LINH TRAN, PROFESSOR OF SPORTS
SCIENCE, PACIFICA UNIVERSITY

HYROX PLAYBOOK

HYROX PLAYBOOK

A PROVEN ROADMAP TO FINISH HYROX FASTER
AND BUILD LIFELONG FITNESS

MARK BROWN

Copyright © 2025 by Mark Brown

All rights reserved.

No part of this publication may be reproduced, distributed, or transmitted in any form or by any means, including photocopying, recording, or other electronic or mechanical methods, without the prior written permission of the publisher, except in the case of brief quotations embodied in critical reviews and certain other noncommercial uses permitted by copyright law.

Disclaimer: The information provided in this book is for educational and entertainment purposes only. The author and publisher make no representation or warranties with respect to the accuracy, applicability, fitness, or completeness of the contents of this book. The information contained in this book is strictly for educational purposes. Therefore, if you wish to apply ideas contained in this book, you are taking full responsibility for your actions.

The author and publisher disclaim any warranties (express or implied), merchantability, or fitness for any particular purpose. The author and publisher shall in no event be held liable to any party for any direct, indirect, punitive, special, incidental, or other consequential damages arising directly or indirectly from any use of this material, which is provided "as is," and without warranties.

First Edition

To my family, whose unwavering support kept me moving when the pace grew heavy. To every reader and athlete stepping into HYROX—may this guide turn curiosity into courage and effort into lasting strength.

Strength does not come from physical capacity. It comes from an indomitable will.

MOHANDAS KARAMCHAND GANDHI

CONTENTS

Welcome to the World of HYROX — xv

1. UNDERSTANDING THE HYROX RACE FORMAT — 1
   - The Classic HYROX Layout — 1
   - Divisions and Categories Explained — 4
   - Rules, Standards, and Judging — 7
   - Event Day Flow — 10
   - Global Standardization and Why It Matters — 12

2. FITNESS FOUNDATIONS: WHAT HYROX REALLY TESTS — 15
   - The Hybrid Fitness Spectrum — 15
   - Energy Systems at Work — 18
   - Strength vs Strength-Endurance — 21
   - Movement Patterns and Planes — 23
   - Transfer from Other Sports — 25

3. KNOW YOURSELF: ASSESSING YOUR STARTING POINT — 29
   - Baseline Reality Check — 29
   - Movement Map: Spotting Your Tight Spots — 32
   - Strength Benchmarks for Your HYROX Engine — 35
   - The Recovery Ledger — 38
   - Choosing Your First HYROX Target — 40

4. MASTERING THE HYROX STATIONS — 43
   - SkiErg: The Opening Stroke — 43
   - Sled Push: Driving Power Without Burning Out — 46
   - Sled Pull: Momentum and Grip — 48
   - Burpee Broad Jumps: Pace, Power, and Precision — 49

RowErg: Rhythm, Reach, and Resistance	51
Farmers Carry: Grip, Posture, and Turn Strategy	53
Sandbag Lunges: Load, Lunge, and Look Ahead	55
Wall Balls: Break Sets with Control	57

5. BUILDING YOUR HYROX ENGINE: RUNNING & CONDITIONING — 59
   - The Running Gatekeeper of HYROX — 59
   - Building the Easy Run Foundation — 61
   - Intervals, Tempos, and Threshold Work — 62
   - Hybrid Intervals: Running with Stations — 64
   - Conditioning Beyond Running — 65

6. STRENGTH, POWER, AND DURABILITY FOR HYROX — 67
   - Fundamental Strength Movements — 67
   - Power and Force Production — 70
   - Muscular Endurance and High-Rep Sets — 72
   - Core and Carry Strength — 74
   - Balancing Strength with Conditioning — 76

7. DESIGNING YOUR HYROX TRAINING PLAN — 79
   - Principles guiding your HYROX programming — 79
   - Choosing your training split — 82
   - 12-Week Beginner Plan — 85
   - 12-Week Intermediate/Improver Plan — 87
   - 8–10 Week Time-Crunched Plan — 89
   - Adapting plans for doubles and relays — 91

8. SMART STRATEGY: PACING, NUTRITION, AND RACE DAY EXECUTION — 93
   - Pace with Purpose — 93
   - Station by Station Strategy — 96
   - Fuel for the Finish — 98
   - Warm-Up That Works — 101

In the Thick of It 104
Decode Your Race: Post-Race Analysis 106

9. MINDSET, MOTIVATION, AND MENTAL RESILIENCE 111
Overcoming Intimidation and Imposter Syndrome 111
Goal Setting Beyond the Finish Line 114
Building Training Consistency 116
In-Race Mental Tools 118
Community, Accountability, and Support 121

10. COACHING, CLASSES, AND INTEGRATING HYROX INTO REAL LIFE 123
HYROX Gym vs Regular Gym: Two Training Worlds 123
When to Work with a Coach: The value of guidance 126
Designing HYROX-inspired classes that are inclusive and fun 128
Blending HYROX with other races: A smarter approach to calendar planning 131
Keeping training in balance: Work, family, and life outside the gym 133
Coaching clients for HYROX: A practical framework for trainers 135

HYROX as a Catalyst for Lifelong Fitness 139

WELCOME TO THE WORLD OF HYROX

WHAT HYROX IS—AND ISN'T

HYROX is a standardized global fitness race designed to measure more than one facet of athleticism at once. It blends running with a series of functional workouts performed between 1-kilometer segments, all tied together in a single event. The idea is simple on the surface: push your body through a continuous circuit that tests endurance, strength, speed, and mental grit. The reality, though, is richer. HYROX isn't merely a test of mileage or a showcase for brute lifting. It's a carefully engineered format that balances consistent expectations with enough variability to keep it engaging across locations and competitors.

WHY HYROX IS EXPLODING IN POPULARITY

In recent years, athletes and weekend warriors have grown hungry for what you might call hybrid fitness—something that refuses to live in a single box. HYROX sits squarely in that space by reminding people that real fitness isn't one skill in isolation. It's a multi-layered capability: you need the steady cadence of running, the precision and power of functional movements, and the resilience to stay present when fatigue mounts. The result is a format that feels both familiar and novel, inviting newcomers while rewarding the most trained athletes.

WHO THIS BOOK IS FOR

This book speaks to a broad audience, and it speaks with you in mind wherever you are on your HYROX journey. If you're a recreational runner who loves a challenge but isn't sure how to merge endurance with strength work, you'll find a clear path forward. If you're a CrossFit or functional fitness athlete curious about a new competition format, you'll discover how your skill set translates into HYROX-specific demands. Coaches and trainers will find practical guidance for guiding clients through HYROX prep, while busy adults will appreciate the structure, efficiency, and goal-driven approach that fits into a tight schedule.

HOW TO USE THIS BOOK

Think of this book as a flexible map rather than a rigid drill sergeant. You can read straight through to build a solid foundation, or you can jump directly to sections that address your immediate questions. The chapters are designed to interlock, so you'll see how the pieces fit together even when you skip around. You'll encounter scalable workouts, sample training blocks, and practical strategies that let you personalize plans to your window of time, your current fitness, and your long-term HYROX goals. Use this chapter to orient yourself, then decide how deep you want to dive into the specifics later on.

A NEW DEFINITION OF 'TRULY FIT'

HYROX presents a broader lens on fitness than many traditional events. Truly fit means more than being fast or strong in one isolated task. It means showing up ready to sustain effort, recover quickly, and perform consistently across a series of demands. Endurance isn't just about going longer; it's about the body's efficiency and the nervous system's ability to keep firing under fatigue. Strength isn't only peak power; it's durability, technique, and the capacity to carry odd loads with control when the body is tired. Speed isn't only a one-off sprint; it's the ability to accelerate and hold a challenging pace when the clock is ticking and the mind starts to wander. Resilience is the common thread—the mental stamina to push through discomfort, to reset after a tough station, and to stay focused when fatigue blurs the finish line.

ONE
UNDERSTANDING THE HYROX RACE FORMAT

THE CLASSIC HYROX LAYOUT

HYROX presents a single, relentless rhythm: eight one-kilometer runs interlaced with eight functional workouts. The course is designed to press you from start to finish, testing not only your endurance but how well you can stay composed, switch gears, and move efficiently between extremely different demands. The idea is simple on paper, but brutal in practice: run a kilometer, hit a workout, run another kilometer, hit the next workout, all the way through eight cycles. The sequence is fixed, the distance is fixed, and the clock never lies.

You start with a 1 kilometer loop that puts your legs into a steady, prying rhythm. The first turn of the course already begins to separate the curious from the committed. After completing the run, you reach the first station and you switch mental gears. The eight workouts stay in order across the race, so the second you step off the track, your focus shifts to the Sled Push with its own demands. You pursue forward motion against resistance, your breathing working in tandem with the machine's friction and your own legs, hips, and core driving the movement. When you're done, you run again, feeling the difference as fatigue crawls into your limbs and your pace wavers. The pattern repeats for all eight stations, a fast and unforgiving cadence that doesn't give you time to regroup—only to adjust.

The workouts themselves form a compact zoo of movement: Sled Push and Sled Pull demand grip, leg drive, and chest-up posture; Burpee Broad Jump tests full-body power, coordination, and the ability to transfer recovery into a dynamic jump; Rowing forces endurance and smooth rhythm, turning output into distance; Farmers Carry requires grip and upright torso under fatigue; Sandbag Lunges challenge balance and unilateral leg strength; Wall Balls combine throwing power with hip hinge and knee control; Shuttle Run elevates speed and turning accuracy in a tight space. Each station is a discrete skill you must execute cleanly, but the magic happens in the transitions. The moment you drop into the next run, your legs must carry you through the fatigue while your lungs try to find a new rhythm.

A critical feature of the format is consistency. HYROX events around the world mirror one another so that a racer who trains for the format can expect comparable experiences at any host city. The fixed distance of 1 km per leg and the identical eight-station circuit give you a reliable blueprint for training and benchmarking. You aren't chasing a mystery course; you're chasing a measurable standard whose value grows as you compare your performance across sessions, venues, and even continents. This is the heart of HYROX: you don't just train for a single race—you construct a repeatable performance template that travels with you.

In practice, the run-station rhythm creates a mental cadence as well as a physical one. Each kilometer becomes a unit—an opportunity to test pacing, to check your form, to reset the mind for the next set of demands. You'll notice that the most successful HYROX athletes are not the ones who burst out at sprint speed on the first kilometer, but those who treat each segment as a controlled puzzle, saving enough energy to tackle the next station with precision. The science of the format rewards smart distribution of effort, clean technique, and the ability to maintain a serviceable pace across the entire course. Training for this rhythm means valuing consistency over heroic single-sprint performance and building the capacity to switch from endurance to power and back again with almost no warning.

For newcomers, the layout can feel intimidating at first glance. The total workload is large, and the fixed sequence leaves little room for improvisation. The payoff, however, is clarity. You know exactly what to expect on competition day, and you can prepare accordingly. Practicing the eight stations in order, within the running pattern, makes the race more predictable and less daunting. The aim is not just to survive the course but to wire a routine where your bodies can handle the sequence, your minds stay calm, and your transitions become almost automatic.

In short, the Classic HYROX Layout is a deliberate blend of endurance and functional intensity, stitched together by a consistent, repeatable format. It is the backbone of HYROX—the benchmark against which every training plan is measured and every race is understood.

DIVISIONS AND CATEGORIES EXPLAINED

HYROX opens the door to a spectrum of formats so athletes with different goals, schedules, and competitive appetites can find their place. The divisions and categories are designed to preserve fair competition while enabling a broad cross-section of athletes to challenge themselves and measure progress against meaningful peers. In practice, you'll encounter four primary divisions—Open, Pro, Doubles, and Relay—along with age-group delineations that help life-stage athletes compare themselves against similarly seasoned competitors. The exact offerings can vary by event host and region, but the core structure tends to stay consistent, giving every participant a recognizable framework to plan around.

Open represents the most accessible path of entry. It's where recreational runners, gym-goers, and first-time HYROX participants test the format in a welcoming environment. It's a space to learn the flow, practice the eight-workout sequence, and gain the confidence that comes from finishing a HYROX race. In Open, you pursue personal improvement, but you're kept in plain sight of the overall results, and you'll find a global sense of camaraderie in the process. The emphasis is on participation and personal benchmarking more than podium contention, though strong performances in Open still turn heads and can inspire future strides toward the more competitive divisions.

Pro is the more performance-driven tier. This division highlights the strongest athletes in the field, often featuring stricter cutoffs, seeding, and recognition. Pro athletes are typically faster, with shorter times, and they compete for separate podium spots or prize structures that acknowledge elite performance. If your training has matured toward high-intensity, high-output programming, the Pro division offers a clear target to chase and a benchmark against world-class peers. The experience is intense, but the field is defined by a shared commitment to refining technique and refining pace under fatigue.

Doubles introduces a team dynamic that transforms the course into a two-person collaboration. In this format, you and a partner share the workload across the eight stations and the eight runs. Some events structure the course so each teammate handles different segments, while others require you to coordinate more evenly across the circuit. The key skill here is communication and trust—organizing your paces, shifts, and transitions so your team finishes together and as efficiently as possible. Doubles is particularly appealing to couples, training partners, or friends who want to tackle HYROX as a joint challenge while keeping training costs and logistic demands more manageable.

Relay broadens participation even further by allowing teams to pool four athletes into a shared mission. In a Relay, each teammate may be assigned specific legs of the run or particular stations, and the baton—or formal handoff in some events—keeps the team moving with rhythm. The team's total time is the sum of all members' contributions, so the emphasis shifts from a single-fast performance to reliable, steady teamwork. Relay is a social, high-energy format that often hooks participants who love the community aspect of racing as much as the physical challenge itself.

Age groups provide another layer of context for comparison and motivation. HYROX usually groups competitors into age bands such as 18–39, 40–49, 50–59, and 60+. These groups are designed to ensure athletes compete against peers with similar life experience and, often, similar training windows. The age brackets allow for meaningful personal trajectories. You can see tangible progression within your own life cycle and compare your gains against a realistic peer set rather than a moving target across a vastly different age group. The age divisions also help organizers present fair podium opportunities and meaningful trophies that reflect a broad spectrum of fitness journeys.

Choosing a division should align with your current ability, but it's also about your goals. If you're newer to HYROX and want to learn the format with a supportive crowd, Open is a natural entry. If you've been training with a clear performance target in mind, Pro offers a benchmark tied to elite execution. If you enjoy teamwork, Doubles or Relay can magnify the collaboration and strategic planning involved in sustaining a strong pace across eight kilometers of running and eight workouts. In all cases, the divisions exist to keep competition honest and to celebrate progress—however you define it.

RULES, STANDARDS, AND JUDGING

HYROX runs on a shared code of rules designed to keep competition fair, predictable, and safe. The rules revolve around movement standards, official reps counts, penalties, and the enforcement process. The goal is simple: every movement in every station must meet a minimum standard of performance, and every kilometer run must be completed in a way that is consistent with the event's intentions. The standardization means that a burpee performed in New York should look like a burpee performed in Tokyo, and a sled push in Sydney should resemble the one in London. This uniformity makes benchmarking meaningful and progression measurable across regions.

Movement standards are specific and fixed. For the Sled Push, for example, athletes must drive forward with controlled, clean form, maintaining a neutral spine and stable core engagement; for the Sled Pull, the same principles apply with emphasis on hip extension and controlled movement rather to avoid overstraining the back. The Burpee Broad Jump has a defined sequence—lower into a burpee with adequate depth, then explode into a broad jump that clears a designated distance or line. The Row requires completing the set distance with consistent technique, no jerky pulls or lapses in form. Farmers Carry demands consistent grip and upright posture as you walk a defined distance with heavy implements. Sandbag Lunges, Wall Balls, and Shuttle Runs each have their own rules for range of motion, grip, foot placement, target height, and turning technique.

Judging is a visible, consistent presence throughout the event. A panel of referees observes each athlete's execution, calling reps as they're completed and noting any no-rep movements. If a movement fails to meet the standard, it is marked as a no-rep, and the athlete must either adjust and complete the rep or accept the penalty that the rule prescribes. The penalty could be an immediate repetition, a light penalty in seconds, or, in extreme cases, disqualification. The aim of the officiating is not to punish but to ensure that every participant accepts the same standards and the same opportunities to demonstrate true capability.

Athletes also have recourse if they disagree with a call. There is a formal process for protests and reviews, and the rules of the event typically outline how to submit a challenge and what evidence may be considered. In practice, most athletes resolve any small differences by trusting the process and using future workouts to avoid repetitive no-reps. The system is designed to be transparent, with clear communication channels and standardized cues from judges that help athletes understand exactly what is required at any given moment.

From pacing of the run to the depth of a squat, from the line you must hit on a wall ball to the turn you must complete on a shuttle run, the rules are a map of what excellence looks like in HYROX. Understanding them is the first step toward confident execution on race day— and the best preparation for turning performance into a consistent, repeatable sport.

EVENT DAY FLOW

Race day unfolds as a choreography of logistics, preparation, and focused execution. Your experience begins long before you step onto the start line, with check-in and bib pickup. The check-in process is designed to be smooth and predictable: you verify your identity, collect your timing chip, and confirm your heat assignment. You'll want to arrive with enough buffer time to move through the hall, warm up, and settle into your staging area. The better you understand the flow, the less time you'll waste scrambling between tasks once the day is underway.

The warm-up zone is a gentle bridge between training and competition. Here you'll do mobility work, short accelerations, and light plyometrics to wake up the nervous system without fatiguing yourself before your heat starts. The warm-up area often features space to rehearse movements that will appear on the course, especially the more technical stations like Wall Balls or Shuttle Runs. As you warm up, you'll keep your eye on the clock and your heat assignment. Time management is an underappreciated skill in HYROX; you'll benefit from knowing when you're up and when to make a final check of your kit and fueling.

Staging is the place where nerves meet strategy. You'll line up with your heat group, you'll confirm your equipment, and you'll synchronize with your partner if you're competing in Doubles or Relay. The atmosphere is intense but communal. Spectators cheer, teammates push one another forward with last-minute tips, and the clock looms large. Once your heat is called, you'll move to the start line and take a moment to settle into your plan. The first kilometer is your opening gambit; you'll want a pace you can sustain for a few kilometers while staying mindful of how your legs and lungs will handle the first station and the subsequent transitions.

On course, you move through each kilometer with a steady rhythm and with deliberate, practiced transitions into each station. The eight 1K runs create a tempo that can be managed with consistent breathing and a measured stride. Between runs, you reset core tension and rejoin your planned strategy for the station ahead. The stations are where you earn your time and your reputation; you execute with precision, then return to the track to accumulate the next segment of distance. At the end of the final station, you don't simply stop; you cross the finish line with a sense of completion and relief, followed by a moment to decompress, rehydrate, and review your day. There are post-race procedures—results collection, recovery zones with stretching mats and mobility ladders, and a cool-down area where you can share your experience, compare notes with fellow athletes, and map your next targets.

If you're new to HYROX, this day flow might feel overwhelming at first. The secret lies in preparation: arrive early, know the heat map, practice the eight stations in the order you'll encounter them, and rehearse transitions from the moment you finish a kilometer to when you begin the next movement. With a clear plan, your day becomes a series of repeatable steps rather than a single jolt of intensity. And as you gain exposure to more events, the day flow becomes less intimidating and more predictable—a rhythm you can rely on regardless of location or crowd size.

GLOBAL STANDARDIZATION AND WHY IT MATTERS

HYROX has engineered a unique competitive ecosystem by standardizing the core elements of the race across every event around the world. The idea is simple and powerful: identical distances, identical stations, identical equipment, and identical scoring systems. When a race in a faraway city follows the exact same format as a race you've completed elsewhere, you gain relevance. Your time becomes a true data point you can compare not just against your local peers but against the global field. This standardization creates a universal test, a global benchmark you can chase wherever HYROX takes you.

At its core, global standardization matters because it removes guesswork. You know what to train for, you know where your weak links are, and you can map your improvements with a consistency that few other endurance disciplines offer. This is what helps athletes set ambitious, destination-worthy goals. If your aim is to break a personal best, you can measure progress in the context of results from across continents. If you're chasing a world-class time, you can analyze your performance in relation to the best in the world, not just the best in your city. The standardization also helps event organizers plan, scale, and compare; it makes logistics predictable and ensures that equipment and layout meet the same safety and performance thresholds everywhere.

For coaches and program designers, global standardization is a powerful tool. It means you can design training cycles around benchmark workouts that correspond to real HYROX demands, then watch athletes translate those improvements across venues. It also supports a more inclusive and aspirational community: because the format is stable, athletes can cross train and prepare with the confidence that their efforts will translate when they travel to another HYROX date. In practice, the global standard acts like a shared language—what you train for at one event translates to what you'll face at the next, and what you learn in New York or London can be applied in Singapore or Dublin. This is HYROX's promise: a truly global stage with a consistent, equitable framework that invites lifelong athlete development.

TWO
FITNESS FOUNDATIONS: WHAT HYROX REALLY TESTS

THE HYBRID FITNESS SPECTRUM

HYROX isn't a single-sport challenge stitched onto a run. It's a practical examination of how well your body can blend two big ideas at once: endurance and power. In a single race you're asked to hold a steady pace for miles or to lift a single heavy thing once. HYROX asks you to do both repeatedly, under fatigue, with little recovery between tasks. That's the essence of hybrid fitness in this arena: the ability to shift gears, to switch from covering ground to moving maximal or near-maximal loads, and back again, without losing technique or control.

Think of hybrid fitness as a spectrum rather than a single point. On one end sits pure endurance—the capacity to sustain a pace, manage breathing, and keep form under extended time. On the other end sits pure strength—

picking up something heavy once, with maximal intent. HYROX sits squarely in the middle, where strength and endurance reinforce each other instead of competing for attention. You might run a kilometer, then sprint to push a loaded sled, then grab a heavy sandbag and carry it across the floor. The transitions matter as much as the individual tasks because fatigue compounds quickly, and your readiness across the whole spectrum determines your race day result.

To see this clearly, picture your body as an integrated system designed to move efficiently, tolerate discomfort, and recover quickly. In HYROX, you're constantly juggling multiple demands: a rhythmic running cadence, the stability to maintain posture through heavy carries, the power to push, pull, or throw equipment, and the muscular endurance to keep quality of movement across eight or more stations. The better you are at coordinating all of these elements, the more resilient your engine becomes. You don't merely accumulate work; you harmonize work with recovery, steering through the tough sections with steady breath, precise positioning, and steady nerves.

The blend also changes how you should train. If you're coming from a pure running background, you'll need to layer strength work and muscular endurance into your weekly plan without sacrificing running quality. If you're primarily a lifter or CrossFit athlete, you'll benefit from building tempo and stamina within circuit-like formats that mirror HYROX pacing. The most successful HYROX athletes don't specialize in one skill; they optimize their weak links while sharpening their strengths so they can sustain a high level of performance across the full event sequence.

HYROX also asks you to manage your body's energy economy. You'll experience a chain reaction: running creates a certain fatigue, which then makes the next station feel harder, which in turn affects your running form in the next round. That's why the race rewards not just raw strength or raw speed, but the efficiency with which you convert effort into sustainable power. Economy here means efficient breathing, stable core, joints moving through proper ranges, and the discipline to maintain technique even when you'd rather abandon it for speed. It's not glamorous, but it's decisive.

This is why you'll hear coaches talk about "hybrid programming" and "integration work." It means training that weaves cardio, strength, and skill into the same workout or into closely scheduled blocks on the calendar. It means using interval formats, tempo runs with carrying segments, and short, heavy lifting repeated in low-volume clusters so you aren't buried by fatigue. It means thinking in terms of systems—the aerobic system, the glycolytic system, and the phosphagen system—and recognizing how they cooperate across a HYROX race.

In practical terms, hybrid fitness in HYROX is about capacity plus resilience. It's about the confidence to know you can hit a heavy station after running multiple kilometers, to hold your form when your legs burn and your lungs scream, and to recover quickly enough to repeat the process multiple times in a single day. It's a holistic fitness philosophy that treats the body as an interdependent machine rather than a collection of isolated muscles. If you plan to compete, you'll want a training plan that honors the hybrid truth: you must train for the when, the how, and the why of HYROX work, not just the what.

ENERGY SYSTEMS AT WORK

HYROX is, at its core, an energy management challenge. Your muscles burn fuel, your lungs push air, and your heart keeps the tempo. The race leverages multiple energy systems in quick succession, relying on a well-tuned orchestra rather than a solo performance. The aerobic system—the body's ability to utilize oxygen for energy—drives the ongoing running segments. It powers your baseline speed, your ability to sustain efforts, and your capacity to recover between stations. You're not just chasing a pulse; you're managing a rhythm, a balance between sustainable effort and the urgent demands of each station.

But endurance alone won't carry you through a HYROX day. The stations demand bursts of power, grip, and muscular endurance that push the body into short, intense efforts. Those bursts lean heavily on the anaerobic systems, particularly the glycolytic pathway, which provides quick energy through carbohydrate metabolism. In a HYROX circuit, you'll experience these glycolytic spurts repeatedly: a heavy push, a quick sprint to the next task, a high-rep carry. The key is to tolerate the buildup of lactate, maintain form, and recover efficiently enough to be ready for the next sprint or lift. Over the course of a race, the anaerobic system doesn't just fuel a few seconds of exertion; it supports the high-intensity transitions that win or lose time.

The ATP-PC system, the fastest energy provider, also plays a role in the very short, explosive moments—think a quick explosive move to get a bar or bag into the right position or to break momentum on a stalled carry. While this system has limited duration, its efficiency influences your ability to initiate movement with control and safety. HYROX doesn't rely on one system alone; instead, it creates a continuous demand map where your aerobic engine carries you through the lengthy portions, while your anaerobic and phosphagen stores power the accelerations and heavy tasks.

Understanding energy systems also clarifies the pacing mistakes beginners make. Some athletes try to sprint every 1-kilometer run and crash on the first station. Others hide behind the running pace, leaving the stations to suffer under fatigue. Neither extreme serves the hybrid model. Smart HYROX pacing involves reserving a bit of gas for the later stations, using a controlled but progressive running tempo, and knowing when to push or ease based on station demands. Training that mirrors this structure—repeated, predictable work bouts with brief, targeted recoveries—prepares you to behave optimally when fatigue piles up.

Nutrition and fueling are equally important in this energy tapestry. In training, you'll learn how different meals or snacks affect your performance at various stages of the workout. Some athletes perform well with steady carbohydrates a few hours before a session; others benefit from a small, easily digestible option closer to the start. Hydration, electrolytes, and occasional caffeine or other performance aids—if used—should be trialed in training first to avoid surprises on race day. The science is less about perfect fueling and more about reliable, practical routines you can repeat under competitive stress.

Ultimately, HYROX teaches you to think in systems rather than in isolated tasks. You're training to maximize the efficiency of your fuel use, tune your recovery between stations, and convert every transition into a stable, repeatable performance. The better you understand how your body uses energy across the day, the more you'll be able to sustain effort, preserve form, and push for a personal best when the clock is ticking.

STRENGTH VS STRENGTH-ENDURANCE

A single heavy lift, performed with flawless technique, is a different challenge from eight, ten, or more reps under the duress of fatigue that HYROX demands. Strength is about peak capability. Strength-endurance is about the ability to sustain meaningful work when your nervous system and muscles are tired. HYROX sits in the overlap, requiring both. The race will reward you if you can produce strong, controlled movements repeatedly, not just a single powerful lift saved for the glory moment.

Consider the mental and physical tension that builds when you have to maintain a hinge pattern with a stacked payload while your heart rate soars from the run. The first mile might feel manageable; after multiple rounds, your hips and lower back must stay in good alignment as you move the same load in a fatigued state. This is where technique, tempo, and grip discipline become crucial. Heavy lifting sessions are not optional extras; they're the baseline for building the raw strength you'll need to protect joints, keep bar paths clean, and avoid failing a station when your body wants to give in.

To train for this, you'll blend heavier work with higher-rep, lower-load movements that stress endurance in a controlled way. The approach is strategic rather than brute. You'll schedule sets that push your limit on time under tension rather than just weight lifted. Short, heavy clusters can sharpen your RPE (rating of perceived exertion) tolerance, while longer, moderate-intensity sets push your muscular endurance to a new level. The pace and rest structure matter as much as the numbers on the bar. In HYROX, you'll often perform high-repetition tasks after existing fatigue, so you need to develop the habit of maintaining form when your sensation of effort is at its peak.

But there's a caution here: you don't want to train yourself into a state where your running or station performance deteriorates because you taxed your system too aggressively in the name of "more strength." The goal is a balanced plan that maintains technique under fatigue. That means smart programming: sequencing heavy lifts with movements that reinforce technique and tempo, using recovery that preserves joint health and neuromuscular control, and gradually increasing the density of work while closely watching form. In practice, this translates to movable, adaptable sessions where you work the intention of the lift—slow controlled movement, braced core, and minimal spinal loading shifts—in every rep, even when you're pushing for more reps.

Ultimately, the debate between strength and strength-endurance isn't about choosing one path. It's about ensuring that your overall engine can both lift heavy when needed and sustain under fatigue when the clock is counting down. This is the heart of HYROX's demand: the ability to switch from one mode to another with precision, control, and confidence.

MOVEMENT PATTERNS AND PLANES

HYROX stations are built around five core movement patterns, each expressed through different tasks and loaded in multiple directions. Pushing involves the exertion you need to move a heavy object away from your body or forward through a short range. It tests your chest, shoulder girdle, and triceps, as well as your ability to set and transfer power from the legs through the core. Pulling reverses that load course, demanding grip strength, lat strength, and the endurance to maintain a steady bar path or rope line under fatigue. The balance between push and pull is a key determinant of how fatigue propagates through the workout, and learning to manage that balance can help you preserve speed on the next run.

Hinging—a cornerstone of posture and spinal health—covers movements like deadlifts, kettlebell swings, or any load that travels close to the body's hinge axis. In HYROX, this pattern comes with a twist: loads often have to be moved quickly between locations, with a compact torso and strong hip hinge that protects the lower back. You'll find yourself hinging when you pick up a sandbag, reset a bag for the next carry, or drive a payload on a sled. Squatting makes frequent appearances too, from goblet squats to lunges and loaded step-ups. Squats train the hips and the quadriceps with a full range of motion that mirrors the demands of repeated hip extension and knee flexion during running and carrying.

Carrying is the visible work of many HYROX stations. The farmers carry, sandbag carries, or suitcase carries test your grip and the ability of your core to stabilize the trunk while the arms are loaded. Leg drive, trunk stiffness, and breathing control all come into play during carries, and fatigue compounds quickly here. Movement in HYROX often happens in different planes, not just straight ahead. You'll push laterally on your way to a station and then rotate slightly to position a load. You'll go from an upright row to a deep hinge in a single glance of the clock. Adapting to these plane changes protects you from injury and keeps your movement efficient.

Coaching cues matter as much as the station itself. You want to keep your spine neutral, ribs down, and shoulders safe, especially as fatigue accumulates. A strong core isn't just a six-pack fantasy; it's a system that resists unwanted extension, maintains pelvic alignment, and coordinates breath with contraction. When drains start to happen, you'll rely on your ability to brace, brace again, and then release with control. That control—integrated breath, stable torso, active hips—delivers the consistency you need across every leg of the HYROX course.

Understanding these patterns helps you see where your movement pillars lie and how to train each one in a way that respects the demands of the race. It's not enough to be good at one pattern; you must rotate through the array of movements with fluency, reducing the probability of a technique breakdown during late rounds when fatigue is high.

TRANSFER FROM OTHER SPORTS

HYROX attracts athletes from many corners: runners who know pace but not weight rooms, lifters who know brute strength but not stamina, CrossFit enthusiasts who love the variety but sometimes lack sport-specific pacing, OCR racers who chase grip and control under messy conditions, and generalists who enjoy the challenge of a well-rounded test. Each background brings strengths, and each carries gaps that HYROX training will expose. The key is to translate your existing skills into the HYROX language: the run/push/pull/ carry sequence, the need to stay upright under load, and the discipline to recover quickly between segments.

Runners, for example, typically bring exceptional aerobic capacity and efficiency in steady-state conditions. They may need to emphasize grip and upper-back endurance, since many HYROX stations involve pulling or holding loads that can pull the shoulders forward. Runners are generally efficient breathers and tend to know how to manage tempo, which translates well to pacing. However, they may struggle with heavy, multi-joint lifts that require a precise bracing strategy. The fix is to inject targeted strength days that protect the spine and shoulder girdle, paired with short, high-intensity sessions to rebuild neuromuscular confidence when fatigue is high.

CrossFit and functional fitness athletes already live in a hybrid space. They have a knack for transitions and know how to treat movement as an integrated process, not a set of isolated reps. They'll want to tune their endurance to carry a load across a campus of stations and to smooth out lunge or carry mechanics when winded. The risk for this group is over-accumulation of high-intensity work without enough controlled, technique-focused sessions that preserve form in the latter parts of the race. A simple remedy is to schedule more steady-tempo sessions that emphasize technique with moderate loads and consistent breathing.

OCR athletes come with incredible grip strength and resilience in less-than-ideal surfaces. They may excel in rough holding patterns and multi-pillar transitions, but the running component in HYROX is more structured and relentless than typical obstacle courses. Their advantage is problem-solving and tolerance for discomfort; the gaps sit in precise, repeatable movements at speed and in high-repetition contexts, especially under fatigue. Training for hybridity means converting that obstacle-specific grit into consistent outputs across multiple rounds, refining step length, contact time, and breath control on every station.

Lifters and strength-focused athletes bring raw force, technically efficient movements, and an understanding of load management. Their weakness often lies in endurance and the ability to hold technique when heart rate climbs and muscle fibers burn. The antidote is to rebuild the energy systems with carefully dosed conditioning blocks, maintain mobility work to ensure safe limb trajectories, and practice the full sequence repeatedly so that heavy lifts do not become bottlenecks or technique breakdowns during late rounds.

No matter your background, HYROX is a platform for translating your existing assets into performance in a hybrid setting. The more you study where your strengths align with HYROX demands, the better you'll structure your training. You'll value the contrast between concentrated, heavy work and distributed, repetitive tasks. You'll appreciate the need to protect technique under fatigue and the discipline to manage your breath and posture around every corner of the race. In the end, success in HYROX comes from recognizing how your background informs your plan and then filling the gaps with targeted, practical practice that looks and feels like the event you'll actually race.

THREE
KNOW YOURSELF: ASSESSING YOUR STARTING POINT

BASELINE REALITY CHECK

HYROX isn't just a race; it's a test of how you blend stamina, strength, and technique under fatigue. Before you even think about the workouts, you need a clear picture of where you start. This chapter is your starting line—an honest inventory that will guide every decision you make about pacing, progression, and what to prioritize in the weeks ahead. You don't need to be a perfect athlete to begin HYROX training, but you do need to know where your baseline sits so you can tailor a plan that fits your life and your current capabilities.

Begin with a simple, repeatable set of tests that gauges your readiness across three axes: running, rowing, and strength work. These tests aren't a verdict on your identity as an athlete; they're a map. They tell you where to invest effort and where you can lean on your existing strengths. The goal is to produce numbers you can retest later and watch improve over time. Think of them as a trend line rather than a single snapshot.

For the running baseline, set up a comfortable, controlled environment. A 2K or 1.5-mile time trial gives you a clean read on endurance running without overextending your joints on day one. Choose a flat route or a treadmill with a steady incline you can maintain. Start with a 10-minute warm-up that includes light jogging, some dynamic leg swings, and a few short accelerations to wake the nervous system. Then race a steady pace for the full distance, not a sprint. You'll capture your time, average pace, and your perceived effort on a 1-10 scale. If the route feels too long or too hard, shorten the distance to 1.2K or 1 mile to keep the effort honest but manageable.

The rowing baseline introduces the same principle in a different modality. Row 1000 meters at a sustainable, controlled effort—goal is consistency rather than speed. Use a smooth stroke with a rhythm you can maintain for the entire 1000 meters. Note your total time and the average split per 500 meters. You'll learn how well you sustain power, how your breathing holds up, and how fatigue shifts your technique. If you don't have access to a rower, substitute a rower-style movement with a cable or band row circuit interspersed with short sprints to approximate the metabolic demand.

The strength tests should be simple, safe, and repeatable. A two-minute push-up test challenges upper-body and core endurance; count max reps with strict form. The air squat test is another easy gauge of lower-body endurance and technique. You'll perform as many quality squats as possible in two minutes, ensuring depth, knee alignment, and trunk control. If you have access to equipment, you can substitute a light barbell or dumbbell goblet squat for a subset of your testing, but keep the focus on movement quality first. Finally, add a pull movement that mirrors the pulling elements of HYROX. If you can perform strict bodyweight pull-ups, do as many as possible with proper form. If not, use a controlled ring row or lat pulldown to establish baseline pulling endurance.

As you complete these tests, record more than just numbers. Note your heart rate, your breathing pattern, and your form fatigue. What happened in the last 200 meters of the run? Did your shoulders cave inward during the row? Was your lower back tight after the squats? These subjective observations matter. They reveal the hidden gaps—mobility limits, technique flaws, breathing inefficiencies—that will ultimately determine how you train.

With your numbers in hand, you're ready to translate them into action. Start by interpreting your baseline against general reference ranges and against your own goals. If a 2K run you completed in 9:40 is your starting point and your goal is to finish HYROX in under two hours, you have a clear direction: your focus should be on building efficient running sustainability and maintaining form under fatigue. If your 1000-meter row time sits stubbornly above six minutes, you'll want to dial in stroke efficiency and aerobic capacity without letting technique slip. If your two-minute push-up test yields 18 reps, you know you have room to grow the overhead strength and trunk stiffness that HYROX demands.

Yet numbers aren't destiny. They're a language you and your coach or training partner can read together. The real takeaway is the shape of your starting point relative to the demands of HYROX: running endurance, sustained power, grip and pulling strength, and the ability to repeat high-intensity efforts with proper form. When you understand this language, you can structure your early training to shore up weaknesses while leveraging your strengths. You'll know what to scale back and what to push forward, what to drill in the early weeks and what to reserve for later stages of your training plan. This baseline acts as your compass. It doesn't write the destination, but it shows you the terrain you'll navigate to reach it.

MOVEMENT MAP: SPOTTING YOUR TIGHT SPOTS

Movement quality is the quiet foundation of HYROX success. You might have the stamina to run and the strength to lift heavy things, but if your hips are tight, your ankles don't bend, or your thoracic spine won't rotate, your form will break down under fatigue. A simple movement screening can reveal mobility bottlenecks and technique limitations before they derail progress. The goal is not to become a pretzel of mobility but to ensure safe, efficient mechanics across HYROX's demanding stations and transitions.

Start with a basic screen that you can perform at home with minimal gear. A dowel or broomstick across your shoulders helps you assess overall mobility and posture. Stand tall, feet hip-width apart, and perform a slow overhead squat, watching for depth and knee tracking. If your heels rise or your chest collapses forward, you've identified a mobility or stability constraint in the ankles, hips, or thoracic spine. Then move to a controlled hip hinge, using the same stick to track your spine alignment as you hinge at the hips toward a comfortable depth. You want a neutral spine and a slight upper-body forward lean without rounding. If your hamstrings feel tight or your lower back tugs, that's a signal to work on hip hinge mechanics and posterior chain mobility.

Next, test the ankles and calves with a simple ankle dorsiflexion screen. Place your foot flat on the ground and gently push your knee forward over the toes, keeping the heel grounded. If you can't get the knee past the toes without the heel lifting, you've found a mobility barrier that will influence lunges, squats, and step-ups. A quick thoracic spine mobility screen invites rotation and extension through the upper back. Sit tall, place a hand behind your head, and rotate the upper body as you keep the hips stable. A stiff thoracic spine often shows up as blocked rotation on the side, leading to compensations in pressing and pulling movements.

Balance and control are equally important. A simple single-leg stance test breathes life into your assessment. Stand on one leg, eyes open, and hold for 30 seconds. If you wobble, or the pelvis drops on the stance leg, work on hip stability and foot mechanics. A light, progressive sequence of ankle, hip, and thoracic drills can address many of these issues without overwhelming you in week one.

So what do you do with these insights? Start with mobility drills that address your weakest links and fit them into short daily routines. Use a 5- to 10-minute warm-up before every session to prime your joints and tissues. Then reserve two to three longer mobility sessions per week to address more persistent limitations. Mobility isn't glamorous, but it's a high-return investment. It improves technique, reduces injury risk, and keeps you moving efficiently for every HYROX station—from the sled to the carries to the final sprint. And because HYROX is a tempo sport, the more you can move well on the first 15 minutes of a workout, the more you'll tolerate the later rounds without decaying.

Finally, turn your movement map into a living document. Retest mobility every four to six weeks, especially if you've added new drills or you've changed your training load. The improvements you see in watched areas often ripple through other tasks, enhancing your performance in surprisingly broad ways. A little movement quality work goes a long way toward preventing stagnation and keeping you progressing toward your HYROX goals.

STRENGTH BENCHMARKS FOR YOUR HYROX ENGINE

HYROX asks you to blend endurance with real-world, high-repetition strength work. Your baseline strength benchmarks aren't about vanity numbers; they're a practical gauge of your durability and ability to grind through heavy work while maintaining form. The following benchmarks are designed to be accessible, scalable, and meaningful for recreational athletes and busy practitioners who want a clear plan to measure progress.

Start with simple, repeatable tests that don't require a full gym. For squats, aim for 20 bodyweight air squats in 60 seconds with strict depth and upright posture. If your mobility allows, progress to a goblet squat or a light back squat to 5RM—four to six working sets with controlled tempo. If your posture falters or your knees drift inward, scale the load back and reinforce technique with a focused movement practice before increasing weight. The spread between the two test conditions—bodyweight only and load-bearing—will reveal both your motor control and your capacity to handle external loading under fatigue.

Lunges offer a window into unilateral leg strength and balance, both critical for HYROX's staggered movement patterns. A practical benchmark is 16 alternating lunges per leg in 60 seconds, maintaining a tall chest and knee alignment over the toes. If that proves challenging, reduce the pace slightly and focus on long, deliberate steps with full hip extension and a controlled return. For many, the trick is not pace but form: keep the knee tracking over the foot, avoid letting the thigh collapse inward, and keep the torso upright.

Pulling strength is a hinge across your upper posterior chain and grip. Six to eight strict bodyweight pull-ups is a solid beginner target; if you can't yet manage that, a modified version—ring rows or bar-assisted pull-ups—will still give you a meaningful measure of pulling endurance. If you're working with rings, set a challenging but achievable target: six to eight strict reps with full range of motion. If you're using a lat pulldown or cable machine, aim for 12–15 quality repetitions at a tempo that keeps your lats engaged and your shoulders safe. In HYROX, your grip and pulling power matter as much as your legs; you'll notice fatigue more quickly in the mid to late rounds, so it's worth dedicating a portion of your training to building grip strength and forearm endurance as a component of your weekly plan.

Carrying work is perhaps the purest test of midsection durability and total-body coordination. A targeted benchmark is a 60-second farmer carry with a moderate weight in each hand. You should be able to maintain a tall posture and stable shoulder position while you walk, without the load causing your torso to twist or your steps to shorten. If you're new to carries, start with a shorter distance and lighter weights, then build toward a longer duration with heavier dumbbells or kettlebells. When you sense fatigue in your grip and forearms before your hips, you know you've found your current limit—and you know where to expand next.

These benchmarks are not final. They're a menu you can pick from based on what you have access to and your current level. The aim is not to check off a list but to establish a credible baseline that informs your progression. As you advance, these numbers will shift. You'll be able to push harder, hold form longer, and tolerate the cumulative stress of HYROX's two-mile march and high-repetition work with more ease. The true value of these benchmarks lies in their mobility: you can re-test them every four to six weeks, watching your strength endurance grow without losing sight of your movement quality. In the end, the engine you're building isn't just about how much you lift or how fast you run; it's about the consistency and control with which you can apply that power when the clock is ticking and fatigue is rising.

THE RECOVERY LEDGER

In HYROX, your ability to train days in a row and then show up ready to perform matters as much as the workouts themselves. The Recovery Ledger is your honest accounting of time, stress, and sleep. It's not about producing a perfect week; it's about recognizing when life's demands push you toward conservative planning and when you can lean into a more ambitious schedule. As you begin this HYROX journey, you may be juggling a busy job, family commitments, and a schedule that feels like a puzzle with shifting pieces. The ledger helps you see the whole picture so you can plan around realities rather than against them.

Start by mapping a typical week. Note all training blocks, work meetings, kid pickups, travel days, and late nights. Then ask two central questions: where is there flexibility to add training, and where do commitments force you into compromise? Sleep deserves particular attention. If your average nightly sleep drops below seven hours, flag it. Sleep quality matters as much as quantity; a rough night can blunt a high-intensity session and delay recovery. If you're routinely waking exhausted, you'll need to adjust the plan by dialing back volume, lengthening rest periods, or swapping heavy days for lighter technique days.

Stress, both physical and psychological, is the other side of the coin. A high-stress work week, a move, an illness, or a family crisis can all spike perceived effort and extend recovery time. The question becomes: does the workout schedule accommodate this stress without compounding fatigue? If not, you'll need to trim volume, simplify sessions, or insert extra rest days. Your response should be honest, not punitive. Treat your training plan like a living document that adapts to your life, not a rigid rulebook that ignores reality.

Tracking is the backbone of this process. You don't need a fancy app to monitor progress—just a simple log that records sleep duration, perceived stress, energy for workouts, and a short note about how each session felt. You'll start to see patterns: certain days consistently require easier sessions, while others can handle more volume. Over weeks, this log becomes your internal forecast, guiding you to push a little harder when recovery is good and back off when it isn't. The goal is sustainable progress, not heroic overreaching when it isn't sustainable.

Recovery isn't a passive state; it's a discipline. It includes nourishment—adequate protein and carbohydrate intake to refill energy stores—hydration, and smart post-workout habits like light movement, stretching, and mobility work. It also means scheduling deliberate rest: one to two lighter days per week where you prioritize technique, mobility, or easy endurance. When you pair your workouts with intentional recovery, you turn fatigue into a signal for smarter training rather than a barrier to progress. This ledger is your ongoing dialogue with your body, a conversation that grows smarter as you learn what works best for you.

CHOOSING YOUR FIRST HYROX TARGET

With your baseline tests, movement map, strength benchmarks, and recovery awareness in place, you're ready to pick a realistic first HYROX target. Your starting goal is not a fixed verdict; it's a working intention that you'll refine as you learn more about your capacity and your life's constraints. The good news is that HYROX supports multiple entry points. You can aim to finish your first race, to improve your personal best, or to explore a competitive result in your division. The choice depends on your starting point, but more importantly, it depends on your long-term motivation and your willingness to train consistently for a meaningful period.

If your baseline tests show you can complete the running and basic movement with moderate fatigue and you're juggling a busy schedule, your most sustainable initial target may be to finish the race within a reasonable time, focusing on clean technique, steady pacing, and reliable transitions between stations. The objective here is to build confidence and demonstrate that you can apply a structured plan to a challenge outside your everyday routine. When your first finish line is in clear sight, you'll be more likely to stay motivated for the long, steady build that HYROX training demands. If you're driven by self-improvement and you have the time to train, you may set an improvement target to shave minutes off your baseline times while hitting the key HYROX stations with controlled, repeatable technique. Improvement targets reward consistency and smart progression—two ingredients in any durable fitness plan.

Competitors may be enticed by more aggressive goals. If your assessments point to a higher ceiling—strong baseline power, excellent movement quality, and the bandwidth to train with greater weekly hours—then a competitive target could be within reach. Even so, the transition to a competitive objective should begin with a conservative plan that ramps up load and intensity gradually while preserving form and reducing injury risk. The intent is not to sprint from baseline to podium; it's to systematically build the capacity to sustain a high level of effort across the HYROX distance and the repeated stations.

Whichever target you choose, anchor it to your baseline numbers and your recovery ledger. Make it explicit and time-bound, and tie it to a weekly rhythm of the kinds of sessions you'll perform. A well-chosen target should seat itself within the life you lead—your work schedule, your family time, your training window. It should feel challenging but doable, and it should leave room for adaptation when life throws a curveball. Finally, re-test. After your first block of training, revisit your baseline numbers and your movement quality. You'll almost certainly find improvements, some areas that still feel sticky, and a few lessons about how your body responds to the HYROX stimulus. Use those insights to tighten your plan, adjust your goals, and continue moving forward with confidence. This is how HYROX becomes more than a race; it becomes a framework for consistent, purposeful fitness that you can carry into any future challenge.

FOUR
MASTERING THE HYROX STATIONS

SKIERG: THE OPENING STROKE

HYROX begins with a measured, rhythmic opening that places your lungs and legs under pressure from the very first stroke. The SkiErg is not a sprinting race; it's a controlled test of economy, coordination, and mental composure. Your body should feel long, not hunched. Your spine stays neutral, your shoulders settle away from your ears, and your core works to stabilize every motion as you hinge gently at the hips and drive with your arms. The goal is to initiate the race with a clean, efficient rhythm that you can carry across the entire course. You want to be the person who finds the line between hard work and wasteful effort, the one who keeps your breath steady while your arms stay relaxed and consistent.

Technique starts with how you approach the machine. Land with a quiet, deliberate catch. Your wrists should stay neutral, your grip light but confident, and your elbows tucked just enough to prevent excess shoulder fatigue. The hands trace a straight path back toward the hips as you rotate from the torso, not from the shoulders. A small, controlled torso twist helps generate power without spiking energy consumption. In practice, you're not trying to out-muscle the machine; you're trying to out-pace yesterday's version of yourself. Maintain a smooth, continuous stroke cycle, letting the legs play a supportive role by stabilizing your torso rather than driving you forward.

Pacing is everything at the SkiErg's opening. Your target is a pace you can sustain for roughly the first third of the race while keeping your breath under control and your form intact. It should feel brisk but not desperate. A common early mistake is to sprint the first half-minute, then fight to recover as fatigue settles in. Instead, focus on a consistent rate of stroke and a flow that your lungs can reproduce eight or twelve minutes into the effort. If you're new to HYROX, start your clock a little conservatively. If you're more experienced, use your current race pace as a baseline and hold it for longer than you think you should. The SkiErg isn't a test of raw power; it's a test of consistent economy under fatigue.

Breathing matters more than most newcomers expect. You want a cadence that mirrors your stroke rate. Inhale on the catch and exhale through the drive, steering energy into your core to protect your spine and maintain posture. If you find yourself hitching your breath or tensing up through the neck, that's a signal to slow your pace and reset. Short, deliberate exhales help keep you relaxed and ready for the next pull. Visual cues—think about a smooth arc of the arms and a controlled, even sequence from the hips to the hands—can dramatically reduce wasted motion.

For those coming from different backgrounds—running, CrossFit, or cycling—the SkiErg provides a neutral ground to teach technique without the overhead of heavy loads. If you're heavier or newer to the machine, you'll scale by reducing your effective distance, lengthening rest periods between sets, and focusing on form over speed. If you're lean and conditioned, you can experiment with a slightly higher cadence while maintaining clean technique. The essence of the SkiErg is simple: establish a reliable rhythm, protect your body with correct alignment, and avoid the trap of turning the opening station into a battle you lose before the race truly begins. You'll carry the consistency you build here into every subsequent station, and that consistency is the real advantage when the course starts to accumulate fatigue.

SLED PUSH: DRIVING POWER WITHOUT BURNING OUT

The sled push is the first real test of leg drive and braced core that HYROX will throw at you after the SkiErg. It's a test of how you convert upright posture into forward momentum without losing form. The push is a symmetrical task: you begin with a stable stance, you drive from the hips and legs, and you finish with your chest tall and your hips locked in place to keep your spine safe from strain. Great pushes look effortless; they feel controlled and loud in the engine, not in the throat. You want to be the athlete who keeps your knees tracking over the toes, whose back remains flat, and whose hands stay off your knees and shoulders. The sled is a giant metronome that demands you match your tempo to your ability to recover, repeat, and accelerate.

The first thing to lock in is stance. Feet about hip-width apart, toes pointed slightly outward to allow your knees to track naturally. Your torso leans into the belt line—not so far that you lose your natural alignment, not so upright that you waste energy fighting gravity. The drive comes from the legs first, then the glutes, and only then does the chest contribute to the pushing phase. You want to feel your hips extend through the stand and your chest rise as you compress the lungs. A strong, deliberate exhale as you push helps stabilize your core and prevents your spine from rounding under load.

Breathing is a powerful cue here. Exhale during the hardest portion of the drive and inhale on the return of contact with the ground. This pattern keeps you from holding your breath, which otherwise drains your midsection and translates into shaky shoulders and a lazy finish. If your pace is fuzzy, aim for a pace you can hold for the entire length of the push without a single burst of adrenaline. You're not trying to sprint; you're trying to migrate energy across a long stretch with precision. A common mistake is to hunch the shoulders into the neck and to pull with the arms, which saps energy and creates tension that compounds as you fatigue.

Scaling is a practical tool here. For beginners or those rebuilding strength, begin with a lighter sled or a shorter push distance, and take longer rests between sets. For more seasoned HYROX athletes, the challenge isn't to yank the sled harder but to drive with cleaner technique at a consistent intensity across the entire length. If you're carrying fatigue from the earlier station, shorten the stroke and increase the cadence while staying patient with the load. The sled push teaches you to respect the tempo—short, sharp, and steady—not the flash of a quick, loud effort. It's about energy management, not exhaustion exploitation. Finish the push with your chest high, hips stable, and the mind ready to transition into the next movement with intention.

SLED PULL: MOMENTUM AND GRIP

If the sled push is about forward drive, the sled pull tests your ability to generate traction in reverse while maintaining a safe, efficient posture. Pulling requires a different sequence: hinge at the hips, brace the core, and pull with the lats and glutes rather than yanking with the arms. The grip you choose—overhand, mixed grip, or a strap—will influence your forearm endurance and how long you can sustain the drive without breaking form. The key is to create and sustain momentum, not to sprint through the weight with a hurried, unstable posture.

Start with a solid, minimalist setup. Your feet should stay roughly hip-width apart, with your weight balanced over midfoot. If you've tied a strap, ensure it sits securely and doesn't ride up with each inch of movement. Your torso should stay tall, your shoulders pulled slightly back, and your elbows close to your sides to protect your ribs from fatigue and improve leverage. The pull should be a deliberate sequence of leg drive, hip extension, and arm pull that finishes with your hands near your hips before you reset for the next step. Practice a steady cadence rather than a max effort attempt. The goal is to move the sled in a straight line with minimal lateral drift; any wandering will cost you time and focus at the worst possible moment.

Common errors come from mismatches in body mechanics and grip strategy. Over-reliance on the arms is the most frequent one. When your arms take on the load, your back rounds and your midsection tires quickly. Another frequent issue is letting the hips rise or tilt during the pull, which shifts the load away from the strong legs and onto the lower back. Both issues steal energy and can cause early fatigue that cascades into poorer performance on subsequent stations.

Scaling options are straightforward. For beginners, opt for a lighter resistance and a shorter pull distance, with longer rest periods between attempts. For advanced athletes, you can increase the distance or resistance while maintaining technique cues: a neutral spine, a steady breath cycle, and a hands- in-hips finish that ensures you stay in your power window. The sled pull will test your capacity to stay present and precise under fatigue; the better you manage both, the faster the next station will seem. It's a dance with resistance—don't rush the steps, just keep moving with intention.

BURPEE BROAD JUMPS: PACE, POWER, AND PRECISION

Burpee Broad Jumps are a battleground between speed and control. They test your ability to compress multiple actions into a fluid sequence: the burpee, the jump, the landing, and the repeat. The standard you're aiming for is consistency across reps, not a single heroic effort that collapses your form and drains your energy. If you're in a rhythm, you become unfazed by fatigue; if you're chasing a fast time, fatigue will chase you. Your job is to keep your core engaged, landing softly, and using the hips and glutes to generate linear propulsion.

Technique matters from the first rep. Begin with a strong from-stance position, sink into a shallow squat, scrub the floor with your hands as you push back, then bring your feet back to a compact position before you explode upward. The jump should be explosive but controlled, with soft landings that minimize impact and prevent your chest from closing down on your airflow. You want to land in a way that makes it easy to drive into the next burpee without pausing to adjust your balance. The jump should feel like a natural continuation of the squat, not a separate event that throws your breathing into chaos.

Pacing is the bridge between efficient technique and sustainable performance. A common error is to chase a burst of speed that you can't carry through the entire round. Instead, break the set into smaller chunks and set a mental reset after each rep or subset. For example, consider 5–7 burpees as a manageable block, then reset your breath and technique before continuing. The break can be short, but it should be deliberate. If fatigue makes your form break down—dropped hips, rounded back, or insufficient extension on the jump—pause and reduce the tempo rather than forcing a risky rep. The aim is to preserve quality in each rep so that the cumulative effect stays fast, not destructive.

Scaling options invite a practical spectrum of intensity. For newcomers, perform burpees with a step-back variant instead of a full push-up and skip the jump entirely on the first few rounds. You can also reduce the range of movement by stepping over an implied line rather than jumping. For experienced HYROX athletes, you can increase the number of reps, add a small penalty for sloppy reps, or maintain the same movement but reduce rest time between sets. The heart of the station is pace with control; the body learns to keep the jaw unclenched and the chest open so that you can sustain rhythm when the fatigue stacks up.

ROWERG: RHYTHM, REACH, AND RESISTANCE

Rowing is a study in efficiency under fatigue. The RowErg is a full-body tempo benchmark, challenging your ability to synchronize your hips, back, arms, and breathing. Your stroke should feel like a single, purposeful motion rather than a sequence of separate efforts. The core of the technique is to coordinate the drive from the legs, connect with the back, and finish with the arms drawing the oar toward your torso. Think about the body as a lever, with the legs providing the force, the back maintaining the hinge, and the arms completing the pull. A clean catch, a strong drive, and a solid finish will keep the stroke smooth across the entire set and keep your heart rate from spiking into the danger zone.

Drag on the RowErg is sometimes misunderstood. The drag factor is not a fixed obstacle; it's a reflection of resistance that you must work through with a sustainable tempo. The trick is to find a price you're willing to pay for efficiency in each stroke. Too high a drag and you'll sink into a slow burn; too low and you'll chase speed at the cost of form. In practice, aim for a rhythm where your stroke rate and your power balance each other. You want to feel a powerful drive that doesn't force your back into a position of strain. Your shoulders should stay square, your torso angle should stay consistent, and your wrists should remain relaxed while you do the work.

Common errors are easy to fall into. A round back or a slack grip will cause you to waste energy and fatigue your lats, rhomboids, and lower back. A too-quick drive with the legs often leads to a sudden heavy breath, a compromised finish, and a late recovery. Conversely, a too-sluggish rate will drain your pace and leave you with little momentum as you approach the later rounds. The right balance is a rhythm that you can repeat without burning out. During training, practice intervals at varied drag factors and stroke rates to identify your sustainable window. Hydration and pacing on race day matter just as much as proper form. Build a mental map of your pacing: a steady base, a smooth upswing when you're fresh, and a controlled return to base as you settle into the middle miles.

Scaling options are dynamic here. For beginners, reduce the drag and/or the distance, and emphasize technique over speed. For experienced HYROX athletes, add distance or adjust drag to challenge your endurance and your capacity to recover. The RowErg trains you to hold a precise rhythm under fatigue, a habit that pays off in every station that follows. Use this station to rehearse your mental algorithm: settle, engage, execute, recover. In doing so, you'll preserve your form, protect your joints, and move efficiently toward the next movement with your lungs clear and your mind focused.

FARMERS CARRY: GRIP, POSTURE, AND TURN STRATEGY

The Farmers Carry is the ultimate test of grip endurance and posture under fatigue. Your hands become the limiters here, but your eyes and spine must stay upright long after your forearms cry out for relief. There's a simple truth: if you can hold onto your mechanics, your body will carry you farther than your grip will allow. Keep your chest tall, your shoulders anchored, and your midsection braced as you walk. A neutral spine and a steady gaze help you march through fatigue without bending until you break. The turns at the far end of the course—where you swap direction—are where you'll often lose seconds. You'll want short, precise turns that keep your momentum intact and your breath under control.

Grip management matters more than you might expect. Chalk can help, but comfort and stability matter more. Your grip should feel secure, not clenched to exhaustion. If your grip starts to fail, the entire carry slows down. A key technique is to keep the load close to your center of gravity so that you don't torque your shoulders or peel your hips off line. Posture is the other silent partner: upright hips, engaged lats, and a core that bristles with readiness. A common error is letting the shoulders creep forward or the elbows flare out as fatigue climbs. Both mistakes pull your center of gravity off balance, increase fatigue, and slow your transitions.

Turn strategy is practical, not glamorous. Approach the turn like a mini-stroke—short steps, deliberate pivots, and a reset of the breath. If you're carrying a lot of weight, you'll benefit from a quicker, smaller turn rather than a wide, momentum-sapping arc. If you're lighter, you can afford a slightly longer arc that maintains your stride tempo without compromising your breath. The best athletes read the course and adjust on the fly: shorter, tighter turns when the path is congested; bigger, cleaner turns when you're in your own lane and can hold a high cadence.

Scaling is straightforward. For beginners, reduce load, shorten the distance, or break the carry into two manageable segments with a brief rest in between. For more advanced athletes, increase load, sustain longer carries, and practice multiple turns in quick succession. The

Farmer's Carry is not about brute speed; it's about reliable, repeatable pressure that you can keep applying without losing form. It teaches you to respect your grip, to honor your posture, and to stay present long enough to finish strong.

SANDBAG LUNGES: LOAD, LUNGE, AND LOOK AHEAD

The Sandbag Lunge tests your ability to maintain balance, control your descent, and coordinate the transfer of weight as you move forward. The load challenges your core and your legs—one misstep can cascade into wasted time as you realign. The go-to principle here is simple: keep load centered, torso upright, and knee tracking in a straight line over the toe of the front leg. A stable trunk and a deliberate pace will protect your joints from shear forces while allowing you to maximize stride length without compromising alignment.

Load placement matters for safety and speed. If you're carrying the bag on your shoulders in a traditional front rack, you'll want to keep the weight high enough to prevent the bag from swinging forward and pulling you off balance. If you're front-loading across the chest, you'll rely more on core engagement to stabilize the torso through movement. Either way, the aim is to keep your hips square to the direction of travel and your knee tracking in the same line as your toes. The movement's rhythm should be a controlled set of steps where you step forward, descend, and rise with a crisp hip extension that drives you back to an upright position ready for the next rep.

Common errors often come from overreaching with the back leg or letting the knee drift inward toward the centerline. The result is a wobbly stance, a compromised knee, and a slower transition back to standing. You'll also see cohorts of athletes who overcorrect by leaning too far forward, which shifts the weight onto the toes and can create shin and knee pain. The fix is balance and alignment: keep your chest open, your gaze forward, and your core engaged so you can press back to the starting position with a strong hip thrust.

Scaling options reflect the mixed audience HYROX attracts. Beginners can use a lighter sandbag, shorten the range of motion, or perform static lunges with the bag supported rather than moving. For intermediate and advanced athletes, you can increase the bag's load, extend the range of motion, or add tempo work that forces you to hold form under fatigue. Either path emphasizes a safe, controlled movement pattern that translates into every other movement on the course. The sandbag lunges are a reminder that the best HYROX athletes are those who move with intention, maintain control, and finish with a deliberate, powerful stride rather than a rushed, reckless lunge into fatigue.

WALL BALLS: BREAK SETS WITH CONTROL

Wall balls blend a functional squat with a ball throw into a single, demanding exercise. It's a test of full-body coordination and the ability to break sets intelligently. The station rewards athletes who master the transition from a deep, controlled squat to a precise toss at height, then reset with the next rep in the same clean sequence. Your technique should be rooted in consistent mechanics: hips descend to a reliable depth, the core remains braced, and the throw uses the momentum of the hips to drive the ball upward. The eyes stay focused on the ball, not on the ceiling, and the breath is synchronized with the movement to avoid the familiar trap of breath-holding.

Setup matters. Position your feet for balance and a natural hip hinge. The ball is held in a way that allows you to deliver power from the legs through the torso into the arms without overloading the shoulders. Your squat depth needs to be consistent; no one está going to score for depth alone, but the movement is penalized for inconsistency. The throw should be a controlled extension rather than a frantic push. You want to feel your hips extend and your arms finish through the target with your core stabilizing you through the moment of release.

Pacing is critical. The most common error is to try to smash through reps without considering how to recover between them. The best Wall Ball performers plan the sets, recognizing when to pause briefly to gather breath and reset form. It's better to take a short, deliberate break than to push through fatigue with bad technique. A simple rule of thumb: if your form starts to degrade—decreased squat depth, mis-timed release, or inconsistent follow-through—pause and reset rather than chase a premature finish.

Scaling options provide a practical ladder for readers of all backgrounds. Beginners can use a lighter ball or set a lower target height, emphasizing the mechanics and rhythm over the speed. Mid-level athletes can perform the same actions with a standard ball and height, focusing on efficient, repeatable cycles. The most advanced HYROX athletes can increase the pace and test how quickly they can lower into the squat, stabilize, and release under fatigue. The Wall Ball is the heart of the course's upper-body challenge, a signal that strength and conditioning live in the same breath as technique and mental fortitude. The better you harmonize the squat, the catch, and the throw, the more consistent your transition into the next station becomes.

FIVE
BUILDING YOUR HYROX ENGINE: RUNNING & CONDITIONING

THE RUNNING GATEKEEPER OF HYROX

Running is the heartbeat of HYROX. It is the common thread that threads together every kilometer and every station, and it often decides the finish more than many athletes expect. The 8 kilometers of running aren't just a backdrop; they are a relentless tempo setter that shapes how you approach each station, each carry, each push of the sled. If you want to move efficiently through the course, you must learn to read your pace and protect your legs for the long haul. The run is not a separate workout you cram in; it is the engine that powers your entire race.

In HYROX, every step is a decision. You'll start with a pace that feels controlled, but you'll need to manage it so that you aren't drained before you reach the midcourse.

The stations demand power, but power without endurance collapses under fatigue. The key is to blend a sustainable running rhythm with bursts of effort at the stations that come next. When the pace is right, your breathing stays steady, your stride remains fluid, and your arms swing with purpose rather than tension. When it isn't, even a small misstep compounds across the course and steals your ability to recover between movements.

Pacing, then, becomes a skill you practice as much as a physical attribute. A steady rhythm can translate into smoother transitions and sharper performance in the working sections that follow. The run is also a mental test: staying calm, avoiding panic when the course winds, and knowing when to press and when to ease. If you treat the run as a critical, game-determining segment rather than a simple means to an end, you'll unlock a level of control that makes the whole event feel more manageable.

Form matters under fatigue. A compact, efficient stride reduces wasted energy. A quick cadence protects your hip flexors and keeps your legs ready for the next demand. A consistent arm drive sustains momentum and helps you stay upright as fatigue increases. You don't need to run with the intensity of a track meet, but you must run with intention. In HYROX, your run is your anchor; keep it solid, and the rest of the race follows with confidence.

BUILDING THE EASY RUN FOUNDATION

Your base is the quiet work that often goes unseen but is essential for the explosive, race-specific demands of HYROX. Easy runs aren't easy because they are simple; they are easy because they enable you to accumulate consistent volume without inviting burnout or injury. The aim at this stage is to build a durable engine you can rely on when the pace tightens and fatigue climbs. This is where sustainable programming earns its keep.

A comfortable, conversational pace is a useful yardstick. If you can chat in full sentences without gasping, you're probably in the right zone. Easy runs give your body the chance to adapt, strengthen connective tissue, improve mitochondrial efficiency, and improve your running economy. They're not glamorous; they're the foundation that makes every other workout possible. The logic is simple: more time spent running in an efficient zone produces greater endurance with less wear and tear.

Volume is king in this phase, but it's a careful king. Too much too soon invites injury and burnout; too little, and you'll stall your progress. A practical approach is to start with two to four easy runs per week and gradually increase total weekly time by small increments. This base should also include a longer run once weekly that gradually extends in duration. The point is not to turn every run into a test but to accumulate gentle, steady stress that your body can absorb and adapt to.

Cross-training can support your base without draining your running days. Rowing, cycling, or an easy circuit workout can add helpful cardio stress while sharing load across different muscle groups. The body appreciates variation, and cross-training reduces repetitive strain that can occur when you run the same path week after week. The goal is consistency, not perfection. If you stay consistent with easy volume and sensible progression, you'll build the aerobic engine that lets you hold form when the course becomes draining.

INTERVALS, TEMPOS, AND THRESHOLD WORK

Interval work, tempo runs, and threshold sessions are the levers you pull to raise your pace from comfortable to competitive. Intervals train your body to recover quickly while producing high-quality running at intensity. Tempo work nudges you into a hard but sustainable zone, the kind you must hold during the middle part of the run to keep your overall pace honest. Threshold work pushes your lactate tolerance so that you don't crumble when the distance and discomfort rise. In HYROX, this trio is your toolkit for creating a faster, more resilient engine.

A typical interval session could look like this: several repeats at a pace just faster than your current 5K race pace, with short, controlled recoveries in between. You might start with six by 400 meters, followed by a light jog for 60 seconds, then cycle back through. The goal is to accumulate quality work while teaching your body how to bounce back quickly. Intervals teach efficiency under fatigue, which is exactly what HYROX demands as you navigate the dark miles between stations.

Tempo runs sit in the middle ground between easy and fast, a bridge that improves your ability to sustain a challenging pace for longer periods. A tempo workout might involve a 20-minute continuous effort at a pace that feels hard but controlled, followed by a gradual cooldown. The objective is to increase the amount of time you can maintain a brisk rhythm without breaking form. Over weeks, tempo work shifts your personal tempo and your sense of what is possible on race day.

Threshold training pushes you toward the edge of your comfort zone where you rely on efficient technique and tight run economy. These sessions are deliberate and purposeful, designed to push your body to tolerate higher lactate levels with a stable technique. Methods abound, but the underlying principle remains the same: stress the system in controlled doses, then allow it to adapt with patience and consistency.

HYBRID INTERVALS: RUNNING WITH STATIONS

Hybrid intervals are workouts that mirror the rhythm of a HYROX race, where running and station work are interwoven rather than isolated. The idea is to practice moving swiftly from one demand to the next, preserving rhythm, and minimizing rest. You'll run to a nearby station, complete a station circuit, then run again to the next station, and so on. This approach trains your nervous system to switch gears smoothly and helps your body tolerate repeated accelerations and decelerations under fatigue.

In practice, you might structure a session around a series of run-to-station segments. For example, run 1 kilometer to the first station, perform a short but intense station sequence, jog 400 meters to the second, repeat, then continue through a mini course of two or three stations. The precise work at each station is scalable, and you adjust the volume based on your current fitness and goals. The key is timing and transition: minimize downtime, maximize continuity, and maintain a steady overall pace that doesn't crumble as fatigue accrues.

Hybrid intervals also emphasize control under fatigue. While you're pushing through the station work, you're not running blindly; you're maintaining a cadence, protecting your posture, and choosing efficient, repeatable movements. You'll learn what you can sustain after a run and a number of high-effort stations, which is exactly the edge you want on race day. With consistent practice, you'll begin to notice your ability to stay composed and productive even when the clock is pressing and the legs are talking back.

CONDITIONING BEYOND RUNNING

HYROX isn't just a racing format that tests running alone. A robust engine blends running with strength, power, and durability to thrive under fatigue. The stations demand fast, high-repetition work in a way that tests you in minutes rather than hours, so your conditioning must cover a broader spectrum than pure running can provide. A balanced approach includes resistance training, power work, and endurance circuits that resemble the demands of the course.

Strength training should be integrated in a way that supports, rather than competes with, your running quality. Focus on compound movements that build hip and core stability, posterior chain strength, and shoulder endurance. You don't want fatigue from heavy lifting to erode your running form or station technique, so careful programming is essential. The aim is durability: the ability to perform high-repetition or high-load work while fatigued without collapsing technique.

Power work—think sprint accelerations, sled drives, and plyometrics—helps you generate the explosive bursts you'll need at the start of each station or during transitional moments. Short, high-intensity bouts tuned to your current capacity train the fast-twitch fibers that respond quickly to demands. Integrate these sessions with ample recovery to avoid overwhelming your system; this keeps your long-term progress steady and sustainable.

Lastly, adding cross-training modalities such as rowing, cycling, or swimming builds aerobic capacity in a different context, protecting you from repetitive strain while expanding your overall engine. Circuit-style conditioning sessions that mimic the rhythm of HYROX can keep your body adaptable to varying demands. The objective is to create a versatile athlete who can move, breathe, and perform at a high level across multiple modalities while maintaining the specific edge you need for HYROX.

SIX
STRENGTH, POWER, AND DURABILITY FOR HYROX

FUNDAMENTAL STRENGTH MOVEMENTS

Strength is the engine that powers HYROX through every station. It isn't a fancy trick but a practical foundation: squat patterns to build lower body power and endurance, hinge patterns to protect the spine and hammer the posterior chain, and controlled pushing and pulling that translate directly to sled pushes, carries, and high-repetition work under fatigue. When you start with solid technique and a clear progression, you set a ceiling low enough to reach but high enough to push you toward your race day goals. This section lays out the core lifts and how they map onto HYROX tasks, with practical cues you can apply in your next session.

The squat is your workhorse for leg strength and knee stability. A well-tuned squat pattern creates a solid chassis for every sled rep and every loaded carry. For beginners, the goblet squat provides a friendly entry point: it teaches upright torso, knee tracking, and depth without the barbell complexity. As technique becomes reliable, you advance to back squats or front squats, depending on your mobility, equipment access, and preference. The key is to keep the movement controlled, the tempo consistent, and the depth meaningful without sacrificing form. When you feel smooth, you begin to push the boundaries gently—adding a bit more load, reducing rest between sets, or introducing paused reps to challenge the bottom position. The objective isn't maximal weight in a single rep but repeatable, clean power that carries over to the station work on race day.

The hinge is another pillar. Hip hinge patterns—think deadlifts, Romanian deadlifts, and hip hinge variations—prime the posterior chain, protect the spine, and improve hip drive, which is crucial when you need to accelerate a sled or hold a heavy carry for distance. The hinge teaches control through the hip drive and the hamstring's role in stabilizing the pelvis. If you're newer to lifting, a hip-dominant movement like a kettlebell swing or a trap bar hinge can be a practical starting point, emphasizing hip hinge rather than pure quad engagement. As with squats, your hinge work should emphasize form over weight and be scaled progressively. Common missteps include letting the spine round, exploding through the hips with a hyperextended back, or failing to engage the lats and core to stabilize the torso. Addressing these issues early pays dividends when fatigue stacks up later in the race.

Push and pull patterns matter just as much as leg work. Pressing movements—overhead presses, incline or flat presses—build the overhead strength and scapular stability needed for carries that demand trunk control and shoulder endurance. Pulling movements—pull-ups, chin-ups, rows—create a balanced upper body, supporting the pulling actions you'll face when returning from a sled push or when gripping a loaded implement for a long duration. The interplay of push and pull protects your shoulders and helps you maintain posture under fatigue. In HYROX reality, you'll often be under time pressure and under load, so training these patterns with controlled tempo and solid bracing matters more than chasing big numbers. Mastery of bracing, stable shoulder blades, and a neutral spine will carry you through the longest, most taxing transitions.

Programming these fundamental movements requires a thoughtful balance. You want enough frequency to build skill and strength, but not so much volume that recovery becomes a bottleneck. A practical approach is two to three strength sessions per week, each focusing on a couple of main lifts and their accessories, followed by conditioning work that respects your energy budget. You should aim for technical mastery first; weight or volume should grow only when technique remains flawless and your recovery markers look healthy. The weekly rhythm should interleave heavier effort days with lighter, technique-focused work and ample rest. This structure keeps you from burning out while still driving progressive adaptation.

Technique matters more than the name of the lift. If you're pressed for time, you can rotate between cycles that emphasize a squat pattern one block and a hinge pattern in the next, ensuring that you build a broad, resilient base without rushing to hit peak numbers before you're ready. And remember that mobility, warm-up quality, and warm-down routines are not optional add-ons; they're the glue that makes these movements durable over weeks of training and dozens of sessions on the way to race day.

POWER AND FORCE PRODUCTION

HYROX demands more than a strong base. It rewards explosive force that can move a sled, drive a carry, and translate into quick, efficient transitions between stations. Power is the interface between strength and speed. It's the ability to generate a high amount of force in a short period, and in HYROX this translates into faster sled pushes, surer drop-offs, and the capacity to accelerate between tasks even when your legs are heavy. Power isn't simply flashy jumps; it's practical, race-specific force production that your nervous system can call up when you need it most. The goal is to produce high-quality force with controlled technique, even as fatigue rises. In practical terms, that means training with intent and managing fatigue so you can apply power when you're fresh and when you feel the grind setting in.

Explosive work has a natural place in a HYROX program. Plyometrics—such as box jumps, squat jumps, and depth drops—develop elasticity and rate of force development. These exercises teach your muscles to absorb and then unleash force quickly, a skill that improves your ability to drive the sled or accelerate out of a station. Ballistic work, like medicine ball throws or slam variations, trains the transfer of force through the upper body, which matters when you're gripping implements with gusto and your core has to stabilize a heavy load. Sprint work—short, high-intensity repeats that push your speed envelope—teaches your nervous system to recruit motor units rapidly, improving your first-steps and the ability to shift from a run into a station with minimal wasted time.

The power training you choose should align with your current strength and your recovery capacity. Short, sharp bouts that do not derail your overall conditioning plan tend to work best. For most athletes, power work belongs at the start of a session while you're fresh or on a dedicated power day where fatigue from heavy lifts hasn't yet crept in. Keep reps low, usually in the range of three to six per set, with focus on quality over quantity. The tempo should be fast but controlled, so you don't teach your body to cycle through an improper pattern. Rest intervals are longer than you might imagine, giving the nervous system time to reset between attempts. Over weeks, you'll notice improved sprint speed, better control in dynamic tasks, and a higher ceiling for your sled performance when fatigue is present in the latter phases of the race.

As you progress, you'll blend power blocks with your strength work rather than stacking them haphazardly. A simple, effective approach is to place power work after a short, targeted warm-up but before any heavy lifting. If you're pressed for time, you can replace some accessory work with a compact power circuit, ensuring that you preserve technique and keep risk of injury low. The underlying principle is clear: train your neuromuscular system to ignite quickly, and you'll notice the difference when the sled starts to roll and the clock starts ticking.

MUSCULAR ENDURANCE AND HIGH-REP SETS

HYROX is not only about maximal strength or explosive power; it is a test of muscular endurance at a high volume. You need the ability to keep great form while your muscles burn and your breathing tightens. That endurance is built through sustained work, progressive volume, and deliberate recovery. The goal is to copy race-like demands in training—longer bouts of work with limited rest—without breaking the movement pattern or sacrificing safety. The approach balances steady-state endurance with occasional surge work to build tolerance to the repeated, long-duration efforts you'll face across stations.

High-rep strategy begins with an honest appraisal of your movement quality under fatigue. If your squats or hinge movements degrade quickly as reps accumulate, you've got more work to do on technique and core stability before loading reps into your sessions. For muscular endurance, you'll work in ranges that push beyond the typical three to five rep strength window, gradually stacking more total reps over weeks. Training blocks will often feature sets that reach into the mid to high range—think sets of eight to sixteen or more for main lifts, paired with accessory movements that target stabilizing muscles and grip endurance. With carries and high-rep tasks, you'll often see repetitive, long-duration bouts that imitate station block sequences: a grip-heavy carry, followed by a lighter, high-volume movement, then a short rest, and back to work. The aim is to accumulate volume with sound technique and sane recovery, rather than chase raw fatigue at the expense of form.

To manage this volume without burning out, structure your sessions with a clear pattern: a warm-up that primes movement patterns; a core endurance block with a few big lifts or compound movements performed in a higher rep range; and a finishing sequence that reinforces grip, core, and posture under fatigue. The rep schemes should be seen as a ladder you climb, not a cliff you jump. Start at conservative volumes, then gradually extend sets, reps, or both as your technique remains solid and your heart rate and breathing begin to steady at the new level. Rest intervals become strategic tools rather than endless luxuries. You'll find that your ability to hold stable torso position while performing many repetitions improves in step with your conditioning and your focus on efficient bracing and breathing.

An important companion to high-rep work is conditioning that complements endurance development without eroding strength. This doesn't mean endless cardio. It means purposeful, race-relevant sessions that feed your muscular endurance without dwarfing your technical capacity. When you integrate high-rep work with strength, you're training the body to tolerate the demands of HYROX—the slow burn of fatigue, the need to keep technique intact, and the demand to keep pushing toward the finish line. And with every extra rep you complete in a controlled fashion, you're teaching your nervous system to sustain performance across the course length, the stations, and the clock.

CORE AND CARRY STRENGTH

In HYROX, your core isn't a cosmetic feature; it's the central engine that transmits force from your legs to the implements and keeps your spine safe under load. A strong, stable trunk defends against injury, improves balance, and makes every grip and carry more efficient. Core strength here includes cranial-to-pelvic bracing, anti-rotation and anti-extension work, and the capacity to transfer power from the hips through the torso and into the carry. That stability is what allows you to resist the pull of fatigue while maintaining posture, keeping your shoulders packed and your hips moving in a controlled arc rather than buckling under load. Core work is not a separate afterthought; it's woven through your lifting and carrying practice.

Loaded carries demand a different facet of core strength. A carry is a test of grip, torso angle, breath control, and the ability to maintain a stable spinal alignment across a moving load. Farmer's carries, suitcase carries, waiters carries, and overhead carries all stress the core in slightly different ways. When you practice carries, you're simultaneously training grip endurance and oblique control, because a solid carry requires not only strong hands but also a braced, neutral torso that resists sideways tipping or rotation. To train this, you can start with simple carry progressions and then incrementally increase load or distance as your core and grip adapt. The moment you notice your torso wobble, your breath escape, or your hips drift, you know you've earned a signal to dial back and reinforce form before proceeding.

A practical approach to core and carry development is to interleave core work with carrying practice. Short, intense planks, dead bugs, and anti-rotation variations lay a foundation for resisted load and help you stay rigid under strain. When you add carries to the mix, begin with moderate distances and lighter loads to reinforce posture, then gradually push the work toward longer distances or heavier weights while monitoring fatigue in your spine and shoulders. It's a careful balance: you want enough stimulus to fortify your trunk and grip without tipping into a fatigue pattern that degrades technique or recovery. Over weeks, this combination of core stability and leverage through carries becomes a reliable engine that makes your entire HYROX game more resilient and sustainable.

Altogether, core and carry strength aligns with your other physical qualities, not in isolation but as a coordinated system. The goal is durability: the ability to withstand repeated demands—grips, carries, and stability—throughout the race. Your core train should be tactile, precise, and practical; your carries should reflect the realities of the competition, where time splits and fatigue are as real as your lifting numbers. A well-rounded core and carry program keeps you on your feet, balanced, and ready to push through to the finish line.

BALANCING STRENGTH WITH CONDITIONING

The most stubborn challenge in HYROX preparation is knowing how to balance the heavy work with the ongoing conditioning the race demands. Strength sessions fuel your ability to move heavy loads, but run-assisted, high-volume work subjects your body to cumulative fatigue. The art lies in sequencing and load management so that strength does not collapse under the weight of conditioning, and vice versa. You want to protect your recovery so your muscles, joints, and nervous system can adapt to both speed and stamina without one piece becoming a bottleneck for the other. The practical takeaway is to treat training days with intention: plan your strongest, most technical lifts when you're freshest, and schedule your higher-volume or longer-duration sessions in ways that do not blunt the impact of your strength blocks.

A straightforward framework many HYROX athletes find effective is to separate days into strength-focused and conditioning-focused sessions, while still maintaining a weekly rhythm that respects rest and recovery. When a single day combines both strength and conditioning, you place the strength work first while your nervous system is primed, then follow with a lighter, metabolic block that reinforces work capacity without crushing technique. This approach helps you push power and speed without letting general fatigue erode your form. The sequencing also informs your weekly plan: you might start with two to three heavy strength days, then add conditioning on separate days with careful reductions in volume or intensity as you approach a race window.

Understanding your goals and your life constraints is essential. If you're juggling work or family responsibilities, you may opt for shorter, more frequent sessions rather than long, exhaustive workouts. In that case, you'll want to maximize quality within each window, which means precise warm-ups, efficient movement patterns, and a calm, deliberate approach to effort. Rest and recovery are not luxuries but a competitive advantage. Prioritize sleep, nutrition, mobility, and mindful deload weeks that let your body absorb the work you've done and bounce back stronger. The goal is to harmonize your strength and conditioning so they exist in a single, coherent engine rather than two competing forces. When done well, your strength blocks prime your conditioning days and your conditioning days support even greater strength gains—and you finish with a stronger, more durable HYROX engine.

SEVEN
DESIGNING YOUR HYROX TRAINING PLAN

PRINCIPLES GUIDING YOUR HYROX PROGRAMMING

HYROX is a test of mixed demands: running economy and strength endurance, skillful station work, and the ability to sustain effort under fatigue. Designing a plan that respects these realities means leaning on a few enduring principles rather than chasing every new program trend.

First is progressive overload. The body adapts when you expose it to gradually greater demand, whether that means more volume, higher intensity, or a small but meaningful shift in exercise complexity. In HYROX terms, that translates to gradually increasing running distance or pace, adding more repetitions or rounds of station work, and slowly expanding the time under fatigue during circuit-style sessions. The goal is to move forward without tipping into injury or burnout.

Second is specificity. Your HYROX week should resemble the race itself in essential ways: run segments interspersed with functional movements performed under fatigue. The exact movements matter less than training the same energy systems and neuromuscular demands you'll face on race day. You want workouts that mimic the pace, the transitions, and the cumulative fatigue of eight stations and eight kilometers or their practical equivalents in your setup.

Third is recovery. The body adapts in the lull between workouts, not during the workouts themselves. That means strategically placed rest, sleep optimization, nutrition that supports repair, and deliberate ease days. Recovery is not a passive break; it is a scheduled, high-yield component of the plan.

Fourth is periodization and deload. A well-structured HYROX cycle moves through blocks that build capacity, sharpen technique, and then consolidate gains with a lighter week or two. Deload weeks aren't signs of weakness; they are the intentional reset that prevents plateaus and injuries.

Fifth is balance and load management. HYROX blends strength and endurance, so too much volume in one realm can undermine performance in the other. A strong plan distributes stress across running workouts, lifting sessions, and hybrid sessions that combine both elements.

Finally, accountability through tracking. You should track runs, station practice, and lifting loads in a way that feels sustainable for you. Simple metrics—pace, heart rate, perceived exertion, and station completion times—give you a clear picture of progress and help you adjust before small declines become big gaps.

Putting these principles into practice means you'll design microcycles that repeat with small but purposeful variation. You'll push a bit harder for a week or two, then ease back to consolidate gains. You'll practice the exact skills you'll need on race day, while maintaining your overall conditioning base. And you'll align every workout with your longer-term goal, whether that's finishing confidently, chasing a personal best, or stepping up to a tougher division. The aim is a coherent, adaptable framework rather than a rigid schedule. This section will ground you in the logic so you can apply it to any of the specific plans that follow, and you'll feel confident adapting your week when life inevitably throws a curveball.

As you read, imagine your HYROX season mapped across three interlocking layers: a base layer that builds aerobic capacity and movement quality, a build layer that raises race-specific intensity and station proficiency, and a peak/maintenance layer that protects your gains while you fine-tune pacing and strategy. Within each layer, you'll weave running work, strength and durability work, and HYROX-inspired circuit work. The result is a practical, flexible program that respects how your body responds, not just the calendar. The path to conquering HYROX is not a single workout; it is a consistent, thoughtful approach to training that embraces complexity rather than avoiding it.

CHOOSING YOUR TRAINING SPLIT

Your HYROX plan will live in the rhythm you establish for the week. Three to six training days per week is the conventional range, and the exact split should reflect your current fitness level, time constraints, and how you recover. A three-day-per-week approach is lean and often sustainable for early stages or busy periods. You'll dedicate two days to running and technique-focused work, and one day to strength and hybrid conditioning. The two-run days keep your legs fresh and your running economy sharp, while the strength day builds the durability and movement quality required for sled pushes, carries, and high-repetition efforts. As you settle into a routine, you'll gradually add another run or lifting session to bring you into the four- or five-day-per-week zone. The more days you train, the more careful you must be with load management and recovery so you don't accumulate fatigue that erodes form.

In a four-day plan you might structure your week to balance running and lifting with a dedicated session that blends both. One model is a running-focused day, a dedicated strength day, a combined hybrid day that weaves run intervals with functional circuits, and a longer, steady run or pathway recovery session. With five days, you can afford two distinct lifting sessions—one emphasizing general strength and durability, the other skewed toward power and high-end work—plus two days of run work that includes speed or tempo elements, and a midweek hybrid session to practice the Copenhagen of HYROX pace: holding up to fatigue under intermittent exertion. A six-day plan can be built around a clear split: two run days with one longer, two strength days, and two mixed days that blend running and station work, with a rest day slotted where your energy is lowest.

No matter the split, the aim is clear: ensure every week has enough running to build your aerobic base, enough strength to endure the demands of repeated stations, and enough hybrid sessions to train the neuromuscular patterns that connect the run to the work at the stations. Start with a comfortable rhythm, then layer in one or two targeted adjustments every few weeks. If you're returning after a layoff or stepping up from a lighter routine, give yourself a few weeks to absorb the new structure before you push the intensity. The end game is a weekly rhythm that you can sustain for 12 to 16 weeks without breaking your other life commitments.

In practical terms, your weekly plan should include explicit time blocks for each workout, a realistic estimate of the session duration, and a plan for progression. For example, a beginner moving into a four-day-per-week rhythm might aim for workouts in the 45-70 minute range, starting with a simple run-and-strength skeleton and gradually layering on HYROX-specific intervals and station practice. An intermediate athlete might lean into 50-75 minute sessions with a regular cadence of two run days, two strength days, and one hybrid day that tests both energy systems in a realistic race simulation. The most successful plans keep the structure straightforward enough to repeat, while the content remains varied enough to drive continuous improvements. You'll learn to tailor not only the number of days but the quality and focus of each session, ensuring you build a robust HYROX engine rather than a fragile, piecemeal routine.

Finally, consider how you recover between workouts. You'll choose between light, steady activity and true rest days based on how you feel, your sleep quality, and your weekly load. The goal is to arrive at each session with a reasonable freshness and the confidence that the work completed recently will transfer to the race day. Over time you will learn to balance the need for stimulus with the need for recovery, so your plan becomes a reliable springboard rather than a source of constant fatigue. The right split—whether three, four, five, or six days—depends on you, but the core idea stays the same: consistent, purposeful exposure to running and HYROX-style conditioning, in a rhythm you can sustain week after week.

12-WEEK BEGINNER PLAN

If you're stepping into HYROX for the first time, your priority is to finish with confidence and to experience the format without feeling overwhelmed. The 12-week beginner plan is deliberately gradual, focusing on building a solid aerobic base, acquainting you with the eight-station format through technique and light repetitions, and establishing a sustainable weekly rhythm. Week by week, you'll increase running volume and station exposure slowly while ensuring your lifting sessions reinforce durability without overloading the system. The plan emphasizes technique in endurance movements and a steady introduction to the high-repetition, low-rest nature of HYROX station work so you don't get stranded by fatigue.

In Weeks 1 through 4 you'll lay the groundwork: two run-focused days to establish a comfortable cadence, one day dedicated to strength with a focus on major movement patterns, and a hybrid day that begins to blend the two together. The runs are mostly easy to moderate with an occasional light effort to spark adaptation, and station exposure is introduced at a low volume with attention to form and pacing. By Weeks 5 through 8 you'll begin to add tempo elements, longer intervals, and more station work that mimics the race flow. You'll train the body to handle repeated transitions and develop the mental stamina to move through eight stations with steady technique. Weeks 9 through 12 consolidate gains and sharpen readiness: you'll experiment with short push weeks where volume is held or slightly reduced, but the intensity of station work and run efforts increases to near-race levels, allowing you to emerge with a clear sense of how you'll perform on competition day.

A typical beginner week might look like this: three run days with one easy base run, one short interval day, and one longer run, plus two strength or hybrid sessions that focus on building full-body durability rather than chasing maximal weights. The runs are progressive: start with 15–25 minutes and add 5–10 minutes as you feel stronger, with occasional strides at the end of easy runs to teach your legs to accelerate. The strength sessions begin with fundamental moves—squats, hinge patterns, push-pull sequences, and loaded carries—that translate into stability and power for HYROX stations. Hybrid days incorporate a simple circuit that pairs 1 km run segments with light, high-rep station work, helping you practice format, pacing, and transitions under fatigue without tipping into form breakdown.

To support your progress, each week will include a deload or recovery emphasis every fourth week, allowing your body to consolidate gains and adapt. You'll track two or three key indicators: feel (RPE on a scale of 1–10), running pace per kilometer during easy runs, and an objective marker such as total HYROX-style repetitions completed with clean technique. The aim is sustainable, repeatable progress rather than dramatic week-to-week jumps. By the end of Week 12 you should enter your first HYROX confident that you can handle the running demands, execute a solid station technique base, and move through eight stations with a disciplined approach to recovery between efforts.

12-WEEK INTERMEDIATE/IMPROVER PLAN

For athletes aiming to chase a personal best, gain a competitive edge, or move up a division, the intermediate plan accelerates training load while maintaining a commitment to technique and recovery. The core idea is to preserve the base you've built while adding targeted intensity, more HYROX-specific intervals, and more deliberate practice at high-repetition station work. You'll maintain two or three core running days each week, but you'll shift some work from pure endurance toward accelerated efforts that mimic race day tempo. Strength stays essential, but you'll shift toward higher effort with controlled progression to avoid overreaching. The plan uses a six-to-eight-week build followed by a peak circuit to rehearse the race-day format in realistic conditions, with a final taper to ensure freshness.

In Weeks 1 through 4 you'll begin to thread more speed work into your running and place a greater emphasis on station practice. Shortened intervals, tempo bursts between runs, and more aggressive hyro-style circuits will be introduced. Your three to four training days per week will begin to resemble the actual demands of HYROX—short, intense bursts that require you to bounce back quickly after a tough effort. Weeks 5 through 8 push volume slightly higher and increase the complexity of station work. You'll practice more multi-station sequences in a row, simulating fatigue and testing your transition efficiency from one station to the next. Your lifting sessions will emphasize durability and power, with a continued focus on technique that keeps you from accumulating wear and tear.

Weeks 9 through 12 are about peak performance and race-day rehearsal. You'll include one or two sessions that replicate the exact feel of the HYROX format: run, station, run, station, and so on, with realistic rest intervals. The pacing strategy becomes a central skill as you practice holding steady splits across multiple runs and using the stations to manage effort rather than fight fatigue blindly. Strength training remains essential, but the emphasis shifts toward fast, resilient movements that support quick resets during transitions. You'll track progress through station completion times, run splits, and the ability to maintain form under fatigue. The taper at the end of Week 11 or Week 12 focuses on lowering overall volume while preserving the sharpness of your pace and movement quality.

If you're targeting a new division or attempting a personal best, expect two to three adjustments to your weekly structure as you progress: more high-quality running work, a few more rounds of HYROX-style circuits, and a careful but consistent uptick in lifting intensity. The underlying aim remains consistent with the beginner plan: steady, sustainable progress that leads to confident, confident execution on race day.

8–10 WEEK TIME-CRUNCHED PLAN

Life is busy, but HYROX fitness can still be built with a smart, compact plan. The 8–10 week version is designed for adults with demanding schedules who still want meaningful gains. The emphasis is on quality over quantity and on combining elements to create high-efficiency workouts that train both running capability and functional strength in the same session. You'll still train three to five days per week, but each session will be carefully composed to maximize stimulus in a shorter window. Expect a lot of hybrid sessions: short run intervals followed by high-rep station work, or brief strength blocks that precede a rapid circuit that mirrors HYROX transitions.

A typical week in an eight-week plan might include a short, fast run day that alternates between easy running and light tempo efforts, a second day that blends a strength block with a HYROX-style circuit, a midweek interval session that pushes pace on short repeats, and a longer, steady run with a portion of station work tucked in toward the end. Weekends might be reserved for a longer steady run that doubles as active recovery or for a full circuit practice that simulates the race layout. The key is to structure workouts so you're moving toward more challenging intervals and more robust station work while ensuring you can recover from each session.

Because time is limited, you'll often fuse elements: for example, a 50-minute session might include a 15-minute easy run, a 15-minute block of 3–4 short, sharp intervals, and a 15-minute HYROX-style circuit with light-scale station work, finishing with a quick mobility cooldown. The plan still uses progressive overload, but the progression is conservative and focused, designed to yield reliable gains within your time constraints. Deload weeks, when included, should be brief but meaningful—lower overall volume, a little less intensity, and a renewed focus on technique and form.

As with all HYROX plans, the time-crunched approach should be tailored to your actual available hours. If it turns out you can train four days per week instead of three, you can retain the same structure and adjust the volume for each session. If a particular week is unexpectedly busy, you can drop a hybrid session and maintain the running and station work you can realistically complete.

The overarching message is that consistency, even with small weekly gains, compounds into a comparable end result to more time-intensive plans. With careful planning and a commitment to your pacing and form, your eight to ten weeks can yield a competitive, capable HYROX performance.

ADAPTING PLANS FOR DOUBLES AND RELAYS

HYROX team formats multiply the tactical considerations and open up powerful avenues for shared preparation. In doubles or relay formats, you can divide stations between teammates to optimize your strengths and minimize fatigue. The core idea is to design a training plan where teammates practice the same movements and pacing strategies, but in a way that respects the station assignments you'll share on race day. For teams, practice begins with clear role assignments. One teammate might own the sled push targets while the other handles carries, or you split the eight stations so that each person has a repeatable pattern of work that they can execute in sequence. You'll want to coordinate transition practice so the handoff between teammates is smooth, efficient, and predictable under fatigue.

In practice, you'll structure each training block to rehearse the relay flow: warm up together, then go through a mock HYROX circuit where you simulate your two-person division, including the exchange after each station. You'll pay close attention to how pacing shifts when you're relying on a partner for part of the work and how your recovery needs change when you're watching your teammate push hard while you recover. The training plan should preserve enough individual work to ensure each athlete maintains a strong personal base: running pace, station technique, and the ability to perform at high volume and under fatigue. Individual sessions can focus on any gaps you notice in your own performance—maybe one person needs more upper-body strength or better endurance for repeated carries—while the team sessions target transition efficiency and communication.

Team preparation also emphasizes risk management. In doubles or relays, the combined load can be lower per person if you share the work evenly, but you still must maintain form. The plan should schedule synchronized workouts that preserve your timing and rhythm for the actual event. It's common to create a shared calendar where station partners alternate responsibility for certain tasks, ensuring the distribution of work is balanced and predictable. And because HYROX is both mental and physical, your practice should include moments of team mental rehearsal—short talks between rounds, reminders to refocus, and strategies to manage nerves during transitions. The payoff is clear: you gain not just physical conditioning but a cohesion and confidence that only comes from training as a unit.

EIGHT
SMART STRATEGY: PACING, NUTRITION, AND RACE DAY EXECUTION

PACE WITH PURPOSE

HYROX is as much a mental game as a physical one, and the pacing you choose before you toe the start line becomes your first weapon. The race unfolds as a sequence of 1-kilometer runs interspersed with eight functional workouts, and the order of those blocks means your energy will rise and fall in waves. The default temptation is to surge on the first run, to prove you belong in the room with faster athletes and heavier weights. But HYROX punishes bravado with fatigue, and fatigue makes everything harder: the breathing sounds rougher, the transitions feel clunkier, and your mind starts to gnaw at your resolve. The smarter move is to pace with intention, to respect the clock and the body you've trained to carry it through eight run-workout intervals with precision instead of bravado.

A practical starting point is to treat the first few runs as anchors, not finishes. You want a pace that feels sustainable yet challenging, a pace that leaves buffer on your legs for later blocks. Think of your run pace as a rhythm you can repeat, not an all-out sprint you can't sustain. This doesn't mean you never press hard; it means you press at the right moments and recover at the right times. A useful mental cue is to aim for a pace you could hold for a longer, dedicated run if you needed to, while still having the awareness that you will encounter heavier workloads between the runs.

Perceived exertion matters more than raw speed. A simple rule of thumb across the early kilometers is to keep the breathing controllable and the conversation with your body coherent. If you find yourself gasping or unable to speak in short phrases, you've probably pressed too hard. If you can hold a steady, almost conversational pace for the kilometer, you're on track. This is not a magic number; it's a felt sense that grows with experience. The better you become at reading the first 1k, the more confident you'll feel about the rest of the race.

In HYROX, the transition from run to station and back is a delicate moment where momentum can be won or lost. The heart rate spikes not just from fatigue but from the cognitive jump of shifting gears. The goal is to keep the engine running smoothly through every shift: you will slow, you'll recover, and then you'll push again. A practical approach is to allocate a small but definite portion of your total energy to each block. If your plan calls for a slight drop in pace at the start of a tough station, respect that. Don't think of it as surrender; think of it as the strategic reset your body needs to maintain quality throughout the next kilometer.

Smart pacing also depends on recognizing the real bottlenecks for you as an individual. Some athletes find the early runs are the hardest because they're fighting the adrenaline surge. Others come alive after a tough station and then pay for it on the next run. The art is in knowing your own profile and building a rhythm that can be repeated under fatigue. That repetition is what converts your fitness into performance.

To build this rhythm in practice, approach every HYROX workout with a pace map in mind. Before race day, estimate target times for each 1-kilometer run, and then adjust those targets using your own experience with the eight-station cycle. Your plan should be flexible enough to respond to how you feel in the moment but anchored by a disciplined objective. The most important piece is consistency: you want to arrive at the middle of the race with a cadence that feels familiar and controllable, so you can ride the wave of the final kilometers rather than crash into them.

The flip side of discipline is adaptation. If you're new to HYROX, give yourself permission to start a touch conservatively and learn the tempo as you go. If you're more experienced, your plan can ride closer to the edge, with a clear picture of when to push and when to step back. Either way, your ultimate goal is to convert your training into a reliable performance: smooth transitions, steady runs, and the stubborn, calculated push that keeps you moving forward when the finish line comes into view.

The day is long, but the mind can be shorter. When you walk into the arena with a well-practiced pacing strategy, you're not just running a clock—you're orchestrating a sequence of controlled efforts that transforms raw fitness into finished time and hard-won confidence.

STATION BY STATION STRATEGY

HYROX presents you with a fixed sequence of blocks, each demanding a different flavor of effort. The heat of the sled push, the grip and carry of the implements, the endurance overlap of cardio-heavy stations—all of these demand not only strength but timing, not only power but restraint. The key is to understand where to push and where to hold, how to transition in a way that preserves momentum, and how to lean into the stations that suit your strengths while protecting your legs for what comes next.

Every station is a test of your ability to couple effort with recovery. Some blocks demand a surge while others reward a steady, persistent burn. The art is in the anticipation: recognizing which station you can attack with confidence and which you should approach more conservatively to ensure you're still capable of finishing with a strong run-to-workout rhythm.

You'll notice that some stations become powerhouses that reset your pace, while others gradually sap your pace with cumulative fatigue. The optimal strategy is not to sugarcoat this reality but to lean into it with a clear plan. For example, you might choose to reserve your strongest accelerations for the stations that have historically high cost and lower immediate return. Conversely, you can identify the stations that offer a relatively favorable energy return, where pushing a bit harder won't bankrupt your subsequent kilometers.

Transitions are the real hidden battlegrounds. The moment you detach from one task and connect to the next is when momentum either collapses or compounds. Quick, efficient transitions save fractions of a second that compound into minutes won't feel long by the end. Practice cut-and-go gear toggles: grip the handles, secure the belt, set your stance, step into your next run. In practice that becomes a rhythmic ceremony rather than a chaotic scramble.

Your station strategy should also respect your training history. If you've spent months building strength and muscular endurance, you may lean more on the heavier stations earlier in the race, trusting that your long conditioning will carry you through. If your endurance is still your target, you might elect to pace the early stations more conservatively, using them as catalysts to maintain your running form. Either path can win if disciplined, deliberate, and aligned with your overall pacing plan.

But station strategy is never purely physical. It's a mental calculus—an ongoing appraisal of how you feel, what the clock says, and how the next kilometers are likely to unfold. Your pre-race visualization should include a few likely scenarios: a strong start with a mid-race wobble, a measured start with a late surge, or a steady climb that requires tightening in the final blocks. Visualize each scenario and rehearse how you will respond, not in a moment of panic, but in a moment of calm and practiced response. This is the essence of station-by-station strategy: you don't chase every hard moment; you monetize the moments that most move the needle toward your goal.

In practice, this means building a simple, repeatable approach you can apply to every station. Recognize your power thresholds, know your recovery windows between blocks, and above all, maintain a resilient, decision-driven mindset that keeps you moving toward the finish line with intention rather than impulse.

FUEL FOR THE FINISH

Race day nutrition and hydration are the quiet fundamentals that enable big performance when the legs are loud and the lungs are busy. HYROX is less a sprint than a sustained test of energy distribution, and the most reliable athletes are the ones who feed themselves with intention rather than emotion. The right fueling strategy rests on three pillars: pre-race preparation, intra-race fueling, and post-race recovery. When these pillars are aligned, your body carries you through the toughest kilometers with fewer chasms of fatigue and sharper decision-making.

First comes pre-race nutrition. The goal is to top up glycogen stores with familiar, easy-to-digest foods that won't churn your stomach. A typical approach is a carbohydrate-forward meal two to three hours before the event, featuring dependable staples like oats, rice, fruit, or toast with a modest amount of protein. The emphasis is on simplicity and tolerance: nothing new, nothing heavy on fat or fiber that could turn into GI distress under fatigue. If you train in the morning, you might opt for a lighter, easily digestible option closer to the start, then a small carbohydrate-rich snack or sip an electrolyte drink just before the gun. Hydration should follow suit: begin the day well hydrated, present clear color, and continue sipping to maintain a light, steady flow of fluids up to the start.

Intra-race fueling is where many HYROX athletes find their edge. The formula is simple in concept, complex in practice: provide a steady stream of carbohydrates and minimal stomach upset to keep energy up as fatigue accumulates. A cautious, practical approach is to sip a carbohydrate beverage or water at each transition, with slightly more sustained fueling on blocks where you anticipate longer output or heavier work. The typical range you'll see in coaching circles is roughly 30-60 grams of carbohydrate per hour, adjusted to your body size, gut tolerance, and climate. In cooler weather you'll lean a bit more on hydration with fewer thirst cues; in heat you'll favor more frequent hydration and a broader electrolyte strategy. Practice your plan during training cycles to identify what you can actually tolerate during movement, not just in a gym environment.

Electrolytes become especially important in HYROX because of the repeated accelerations, heavy lifting, and sustained sweating. They help maintain fluid balance and muscle function when the pace remains high throughout the race. You don't need to chase every electrolyte supplement, but you should understand your sweat rate and adjust accordingly. A practical tactic is to drink small amounts consistently and to adjust based on hydration cues—urine color, thirst, and how your stomach feels. You might find it useful to vary your intake based on the block's characteristics: lighter, more frequent sips in hotter climates; slightly larger, slower sips when the body isn't heating up as quickly.

Post-race recovery nutrition is a deliberate act of repair. Your first meal should combine carbohydrates to replenish energy stores with protein to kick-start muscle repair. A practical window is within the first hour after crossing the line, though the exact timing will depend on your appetite. Hydration continues to play a critical role—resume fluids, including electrolytes, to rehydrate and support recovery processes. The post-race window is also about psychological restoration: a simple protein-rich snack or meal can mark a clean break from the day's stress and prepare you for your next training cycle.

Having a robust fueling plan is not about a single rule; it's about consistency, testing, and customization. Your body is your instrument, and food and fluids are the fuel you feed it to keep it singing through the whole course. Build confidence in fueling by practicing in training with the same foods and timing you plan to use on race day. You'll soon learn what your stomach tolerates, how your energy feels at different points in the course, and how to ride the wave from start to finish with less drama and more control.

WARM-UP THAT WORKS

In HYROX, the warm-up is not a formality; it's a performance mode. The day is cold or warm, loud or quiet, and your warm-up should be as much about preparing the nervous system as it is about priming the muscles. A well-structured warm-up reduces the risk of cramps, primes movement patterns, and sets the psychological tone for race day. Think of the warm-up as a rehearsal for the first kilometer and the first station, a chance to dial in rhythm, mobility, and readiness so you don't stumble when the gun sounds.

A practical warm-up starts with a light, general movement to wake the joints and raise the temperature. An easy jog or cycle for eight to twelve minutes gets the body warm without fatiguing the legs. After that, target dynamic mobility: ankle circles and calf raises to prep the lower limbs; hip openers, leg swings, and thoracic rotations to prepare the core and spinal mechanics. The goal is to loosen and activate the body in a way that translates to the demands of both running and station work. Then move into movement-specific activation: glute bridges or clamshells to wake the hips, scapular pushups or banded pulls for the shoulders, and light troubleshooting drills that mirror the actions of the stations you'll encounter.

The heart of the warm-up is a short, purposeful sequence that mirrors the intensity of the early blocks without exhausting you. A few short accelerations help tune your nervous system to the speed of your planned first kilometer, while a quick movement prep drill—think a few reps of a bodyweight thruster pattern or a light sandbag carry—tunes the muscles you'll lean on immediately after the start. It's not about cranking up your energy; it's about waking up the engine and making sure your form carries over under load.

This routine should be accessible, repeatable, and portable. You'll want something you can run through quickly in the warm-up area, whether you're at a packed stadium or a smaller competition floor. The more you can practice this flow during training, the more automatic it becomes on race day. When you know exactly what you'll do, you spend less mental energy worrying about the warm-up and more energy on performance, on pacing, and on the undeniable focus HYROX requires.

Finally, add a quick couple of checks before you start: ensure your shoes are tied correctly and your equipment is secure, and take a moment to set your race-day intention. Picture the rhythm you want to bring to the first kilometer, the smooth transition you'll execute into the first station, and the calm, practical decisions you'll rely on when fatigue starts to press in. A strong warm-up is the bridge between preparation and execution, a small ritual with the power to transform how you perform once the clock starts.

In short, your warm-up should feel like you're stepping into your own body's best version. It should give you confidence, mobility, and control. It should remind you that you belong here, that you've trained for this, and that you'll be ready when the first kilometer begins. That readiness is what shapes early success and sets the tone for every choice you'll make from start to finish.

IN THE THICK OF IT

HYROX is a test of staying power, and in-race problem solving is where many athletes earn their finish time. You will face cramps, fatigue, sleepiness around the eyes of your mind, and the occasional equipment hiccup. You will also face that stubborn, inner voice that tells you it might be easier to stop than to push. The way you respond to these pressures is what separates medal contenders from finishers. You don't just fight the clock—you learn to manage the clock's mood as it talks back to you during the day's longest segments.

Cramps are the most notorious mid-race bugaboo. They don't announce themselves with a beacon; they creep in from cornering fatigue, mismanaged hydration, or missed electrolytes. When cramps begin, your instinct must be to soften the immediate demand, settle the breathing into a steady rhythm, and adjust your expectations for that block without surrendering your overall plan. A practical approach is to lower your pace just enough to loosen the cramping muscles and then re-engage with a controlled but persistent effort. It's a balancing act between relief and progression—and you must practice this balance in training so you can apply it effectively on race day.

Mental dips are another frequent challenge. The mid-race wall is real, but it's also a moment you can reclaim with a few cognitive tools. One trusted strategy is to break the race into manageable segments—short, clear targets that you can accomplish with a single breath or a single step. Inhale for four counts, exhale for four. Count your strides until your mind stops wandering, then re-anchor with a small, concrete task like securing your posture or maintaining a consistent arm drive. You don't need big mental epiphanies; you need a reliable routine that anchors your attention to the present moment and stops the slide toward fatigue.

Equipment issues present a different type of problem, one you have some control over with preparation and quick thinking. If a belt slips, a strap loosens, or a handle rubs, you can often adjust on the fly and continue with minimal time loss. The key here is to stay calm and apply your contingency plan with speed and precision. Practice contingencies in training so you're not surprised by minor failures. You might implement a quick fix, switch hands, or temporarily simplify the grip pattern to preserve your form and momentum.

The fatigue that comes with repeated blocks tests your decision-making. The clearer your decision rules, the less your mind will waffle under pressure. Some athletes create a simple if-then framework: if my pace drops by a certain percent or if my breathing becomes too labored, I adjust the next block's pace and the intensity of the upcoming station. Others rely on a health-check mental cue: if you can still speak in short phrases, you're still in control; if you can't, you should recalibrate to protect your finishing time.

In-race decision making is also about knowing when to push and when to conserve. If a particular station aligns with your strengths, you may attack it to maximize turnover when fatigue is still low. If a station is notorious for draining you, you may approach it with a plan to minimize the energy cost while still meeting your required output. The most successful strategies do not abandon pace control when fatigue rises; they adjust the plan with intention and keep moving forward. This is not surrender; it is tactical optimization under pressure.

Every HYROX race offers a set of challenges, and your response to each is a reflection of your preparation. The more you train to recognize, anticipate, and respond to these moments, the more your performance will resemble the best version of your potential. Your in-race problem solving is the practical application of your training—an ongoing negotiation between your body's limits and your mind's resolve, executed rather than hoped for.

DECODE YOUR RACE: POST-RACE ANALYSIS

The race ends, but the real work begins when you step away from the arena and start translating experience into improvement. Post-race analysis is where your training plan lands its payoff, where subtle insights become actionable changes that compound into better performances in the next cycle. The goal isn't to relive the race endlessly but to extract the answers you need to train smarter, not just harder. A thoughtful post-race review helps you understand what you did well, where you lost time, and how to adjust your plan so the next HYROX event is a step forward rather than a replay of the same mistakes.

Begin with the basics: your overall finish time, your pacing across the eight runs, your performance in each station, and how quickly you recovered in the minutes immediately after the finish. If you have access to split data, study where your pace dropped or where you held firm. Look for patterns: did you fade late in the second half? Was your initial pace more aggressive than your endurance could sustain? Did you perform better after certain stations due to a well-timed nutrition and hydration plan? The goal is to map your energy systems across the race. Running sections should reveal your aerobic efficiency; station sections will highlight your strength endurance and technique under fatigue.

Journaling is a simple but powerful tool in this process. Write a few lines about how you felt at different points, what you ate, how much you drank, and how your equipment behaved. Note the moments when you felt most confident and the moments when your form started to crumble. Your notes should be concrete enough to guide your next training block: did you require more upper-body durability? Do you need to work on your grip or your core stability? Did you manage hydration and electrolytes the way you planned, or did you stray into gut discomfort or thirst? The more precise your notes, the more precise your plan will become.

Translate the day's data into a practical cycle plan. You might decide to push a little more on the early blocks, then back off to preserve running form for the finish, or you may opt to strengthen your fueling and hydration strategy for the next event because your stomach felt unsettled in the later miles. The improvements you choose should be measurable and time-bound. For example, you could aim to improve your average pace on the runs by a certain margin, reduce the time spent on transitions by ten seconds per block, or complete the final station with identical or nearly identical effort to the first station.

Another critical step is external feedback. Decompress after the race with a quick debrief from a coach or a training partner who understands HYROX demands. An outside perspective helps identify blind spots that you miss when analyzing your own performance. You can also revisit your training plan to reflect your current strength and conditioning target. The post-race period is a natural time to revisit your goals—whether you're training to finish your first HYROX, chase a time, or simply enjoy the process of becoming a more capable hybrid athlete.

The long-term payoff of post-race analysis is a feedback loop that makes you better, faster, and more resilient with every hull. You'll translate the fatigue you felt on race day into precise actions: more defined training cycles, refined nutrition strategies, improved pacing, and a more intuitive sense of your own body's signals. In this way, HYROX becomes less a one-off challenge and more a catalyst for ongoing growth—a framework that helps busy people in the real world develop not just a stronger body, but a stronger approach to life and training.

NINE
MINDSET, MOTIVATION, AND MENTAL RESILIENCE

OVERCOMING INTIMIDATION AND IMPOSTER SYNDROME

Intimidation is a natural companion when you first step toward HYROX. The race format is a blend of endurance running and functional stations, and that pairing creates a demanding image in your mind. It's easy to feel outmatched watching athletes who seem to flatline on pace and crush each station with effortless efficiency. The first reflex can be self-critique: maybe you are not quite fit enough, not fast enough, not tough enough for the floor. This is not a character flaw. It's a signal that you are entering a new domain, and new domains demand time, curiosity, and deliberate practice.

Imposter feelings are common among recreational runners and gym-goers who are expanding into hybrid formats. The thought that you will be exposed as not belonging can be loud, especially in the early weeks of training when improvements feel small and the work feels unfinished. Rather than trying to silence that voice, we can reframe it. Instead of treating the fear as a verdict on your worth, treat it as information about the next practical step. The key is to translate nerves into a plan you can execute. When you encounter that inner whisper, respond with a concrete action: plan a small, doable improvement, confirm a training habit, or practice a mental cue that helps you regain balance.

A practical way to neutralize the fear is to anchor your self-belief in *process competence* rather than static outcomes. HYROX is built to be learned: you can study the stations, refine your technique, and rehearse your transitions. Track what you can control—your warmups, your fueling, your pacing in the early miles, your grip on the equipment, the cadence of your steps—while letting the exact finish time remain a variable you influence, not a verdict that defines you. When you begin to doubt, remind yourself of small wins from your week: finishing a tough interval set, maintaining form on a fatigue-laced run, or successfully completing a practice station with clean technique. These micro victories compound into confidence rather than residual uncertainty.

Another powerful tool is *visualization* without magical promises. Imagine arriving at the competition, performing in the warmup area with calm feet and a steady breath, stepping onto the floor with a plan that feels familiar. See yourself moving through each station with technique that you have practiced in training, and feel the sense of mastery that comes from knowing you have done the work. You don't need to pretend you feel fearless; you need to cultivate a robust, workmanlike mindset that says, I will show up, I will execute the plan, and I will use the nerves as a signal to sharpen focus rather than a reason to retreat.

The last component is a safety net of support. Identity is strengthened not by solitary grind but by the people you share the journey with. A training partner, a coach, or a small group can reflect back your progress in a way you cannot see on your own. When fear surfaces, it can be softened by hearing someone else say, you did that workout yesterday, that shows you are capable of more. Surrounded by a team that believes in your steady improvement, the fear loses its sting and becomes a trusted companion that reminds you to keep moving forward. In HYROX as in life, you don't win by erasing fear; you win by learning to function alongside it and letting your deliberate practice do the heavy lifting.

As you move forward, treat intimidation as a signal to sharpen your plan, not a verdict about your identity. You belong here because you chose to prepare for this moment. Your worth is not measured by a single race finish or a mythical standard of fitness; it's demonstrated by the daily choices that mount up, brick by brick, toward something you want more than your fear. The mental edge you cultivate in these early steps will outlive any single event and transform your approach to training, racing, and life.

GOAL SETTING BEYOND THE FINISH LINE

HYROX is not only a test of how fast you can finish a race but also a test of how you live with intention over the weeks, months, and seasons that lead to it. The best-goaled athletes are not chasing a single moment in time; they are engineering a path that sustains motivation, builds capability, and protects momentum when life gets loud. In this chapter, we lean into two kinds of goals: process-based and performance-based. Process goals anchor daily decisions. They are the little commitments you make to how you train, sleep, fuel, and recover. Performance goals capture the direction you want to head on race day, such as finishing under a target time or completing the course with a certain level of steadiness. The strongest plan blends both, allowing the process to steer behavior while a performance target keeps the bigger picture in view.

Process-based goals create a reliable muscle of habit. A practical weekly rhythm becomes your backbone: two focused run sessions that build speed and endurance, two sessions devoted to HYROX stations and technique work, and a couple of lighter days that emphasize mobility and restful recovery. The daily choices—going to bed earlier, choosing nutrient-dense meals, showing up for a pre-dawn session—accumulate into measurable progress. These goals are resilient, too. If you miss a session, you have room to recalibrate without sacrificing the entire plan. The aim is not perfection but *consistency plus intention*.

Performance-based goals function as the compass. They help you answer the question of why you train as hard as you do. They might be modest, like shaving ten seconds off a previous interval time or adding five extra reps to a station sequence when you're fatigued. They could be more strategic, such as maintaining a steady pace for the first two-thirds of the race or refining your transition routine so you waste minimal time between stations. The trick is to keep these targets realistic and specific. A performance goal should be something you can influence through training, not a distant, ambiguous aspiration. And crucially, you should be prepared to adjust it in response to life's realities—an afternoon meeting, a family emergency, a minor injury. Goal setting in HYROX is a living process, not a fixed decree.

To keep motivation high, tie your goals to meaningful reasons beyond competition alone. Maybe HYROX is a vehicle to improve your health for your kids, or to demonstrate to a busy professional brain that you can lead with discipline and grit. Perhaps your purpose is to model consistency for a friend who is starting their own journey. By connecting goals to values—health, longevity, vitality, and reliability—you create emotional leverage that makes daily actions feel worthwhile even on days when the workout sounds hard. When you lose motivation, revisit your why, adjust your process goals to match your current life, and let the performance target guide you back to the path with clarity and energy.

Finally, make your goals visible, but flexible. Write them in a notebook or a digital tracker, but keep them accessible in your daily life. Place reminders in your training space that reflect both process and performance aims. The objective is simple: to design a march forward that you can actually carry out, day after day, week after week, with enough reserve to stay resilient when life presses in. It is in this sustainable cadence that mindset helps leadership the body toward HYROX success without burning out or losing the joy of the journey.

BUILDING TRAINING CONSISTENCY

Consistency is the quiet engine behind every HYROX improvement. It is less about heroic bursts of effort and more about the long story of repeatable, reliable action. The most successful HYROX athletes are those who show up more often than they miss, who build workouts into the fabric of daily life, and who treat training as a nonnegotiable routine rather than a best-effort exception to their week. The beauty of consistency is that small, steady steps compound. A simple, repeatable plan that you can execute even when energy is low or time is tight will produce far greater results than sporadic, high-intensity bursts that burn you out.

A practical path to consistency begins with environment design. If you train in the morning, prepare your gear the night before. If you use the gym after work, arrange your bag, shoes, and workouts so everything is ready to go the moment you walk in. Lower the activation energy for training by creating one simple ritual that signals it is time to move. The ritual could be a specific warm-up sequence, a short mobility routine, or simply putting on your training shoes in a chosen spot. The point is to reduce friction between intention and action so you can rely on momentum when motivation wanes.

Habit stacking offers another powerful lever. Pair a dependable habit you already perform with a HYROX session. For example, you can attach a 10-minute mobility block to the end of your workday routine or combine a short mobility dose with a hydration reminder. Once a habit system is in place, the body learns that training is a natural extension of other daily activities, not a radical interruption. When life becomes busy or stressful, these embedded routines keep you on track because they require less mental energy to initiate.

Accountability is the bridge between good intentions and real outcomes. A partner, a small group, or a coach can hold a steady line of accountability while you also hold space for self-compassion. You might schedule a weekly check-in with a friend who shares HYROX goals, or join a club where members share both workouts and progress. The accountability relationship does not just push you to train; it also normalizes the ups and downs of the journey. You learn to celebrate the small wins, to acknowledge missed sessions without judgment, and to pivot quickly back toward your plan. In this way, accountability becomes a source of community and resilience rather than pressure.

Consistency is built in layers: predictable scheduling, minimal friction, purposeful habit stacking, and a supportive network. When these elements align, the routine stops feeling like a burden and starts feeling like your natural tempo. Your body adapts, your mind grows steadier, and your HYROX training becomes less about chasing a single peak and more about living in a durable, capable state that you can sustain long after the race is over.

IN-RACE MENTAL TOOLS

HYROX asks you to endure a pain threshold as you move through a sequence of physical challenges. The mental tools you carry into the floor and the run can either soften that discomfort or let it sharpen your focus. The first tool is self-talk. The moment discomfort rises, you can acknowledge it without giving it power. Simple, grounded phrases work best when you are fatigued and the mind starts to wander. Tell yourself that the body can work through the current demand, that pace is sustainable if you stay relaxed, that form will hold if you breathe and relax the shoulders. Self-talk is not about pretending the hurt isn't there; it's about steering attention back to controllable elements of the task and maintaining a calm, purposeful rhythm.

Chunking is another essential technique. Rather than fixating on the total distance or the full set, you break the performance into manageable blocks. The floor may feel like a single, long interval, but you approach it as a series of segments: a start cue, a rhythm to establish, a sequence to complete, a transition to finish cleanly. Each chunk is a tiny win that you accumulate, and the cumulative effect of completing multiple chunks is a robust sense of momentum. In practice, chunking becomes a mental map that allows you to measure progress even when the body demands rest.

Focus cues are like lighthouse beams in fog. Pick a couple of sensory or technical cues to anchor your attention. A cue could be the rhythm of your breath, the cadence of your steps, the grip on the bar, or the alignment of your hips with your ankles. Rehearse these cues during training so in race day they act like automatic anchors. In moments of rising discomfort, a practiced cue can pull you back from spiraling thoughts to the present task. A common strategy is to tether your cue to a moment of neutral or positive emotion—knowing you can return to calm focus forms a protective shield against the surge of fatigue.

Breathing is not a mere physiological function; it is a tool for regulating the nervous system under stress. You can employ a steady, controlled breathing pattern to maintain oxygen delivery and keep muscular tension in check. A simple approach is a relaxed inhalation through the nose, followed by a measured exhale through the mouth, coordinated with a light tempo of movement. Practiced in training, this breathing pattern reduces the sensation of breathlessness and preserves mental clarity when intervals become brutal. On race day, your breathing becomes the bridge between effort and composure, and this bridge is built in the hours you spend practicing it.

The final mental tool is preparation for the inevitable discomfort. You do not train to eliminate pain; you train to function amid it. Rehearse the floor, the carries, and the final push as if they are pieces of a single composition, each moment building upon the last. Rehearsal is the art of arriving at the floor with a plan, maintaining a steady mind through the tough segments, and exiting with a clear path toward the next station. The more you practice these mental cadences, the more they become second nature when fatigue strikes on race day. In HYROX, your mental toolkit is a precision instrument, honed by thoughtful drills in training and deployed with confidence during competition.

COMMUNITY, ACCOUNTABILITY, AND SUPPORT

The path to HYROX excellence is rarely a solitary journey. You benefit enormously from the leverage of community, where shared purpose creates a force field against excuses and a space where growth can be observed, celebrated, and learned from. Training with others—whether in a small group, a club, or a class—provides accountability without judgment. When someone else shows up for a workout, the chance you will skip it diminishes. The mere presence of a partner can transform a rough session into a constructive one, simply because you are answering to someone besides yourself. The social energy of a group can transform fear into curiosity and curiosity into disciplined action.

There is profound value in aligning with a coach or a mentor who understands HYROX structure and the psychology of performance. A coach can translate your goals into a realistic training plan, adapt the plan to your life constraints, and keep you honest about progress. The right guidance minimizes wasted effort, helps you spot compensations that creep into your form, and ensures you are progressing safely toward your race day. Coaches can also help you interpret data from training—the numbers, the durations, the intensity zones—so that every session contributes to a coherent, goal-aligned narrative rather than a collection of isolated workouts.

Online communities offer a different but equally powerful form of support. Visibility, shared stories, and tips from athletes at varied levels can inspire and inform. In online spaces, you can exchange quick feedback about stations, gear choices, fueling strategies, and recovery routines. Yet even in digital communities you want to cultivate a culture of constructive commentary and mutual encouragement. Positive peer influence boosts adherence and resilience, especially when real life challenges make consistency harder than expected.

Training partners, clubs, and online communities together form a web of accountability and belonging. That network gives you a home base for honest reflection on what's working and what isn't, and it provides energy for the days when motivation wavers. You do not need to endure HYROX in isolation; you can welcome the shared path of people who cheer your progress, hold you to your commitments, and celebrate your wins, large or small. In this chapter, we recognize that HYROX is as much a social exchange as a physical challenge, and we lean into that reality as a cornerstone of sustainable success.

TEN
COACHING, CLASSES, AND INTEGRATING HYROX INTO REAL LIFE

HYROX GYM VS REGULAR GYM: TWO TRAINING WORLDS

HYROX training sits at the intersection of endurance and functional strength, and that often means the gym environment itself becomes part of the program. A HYROX facility tends to feel like a purpose-built arena: sleds, sandbags, prowlers, rowers, and weight plates arranged with how-to guides and a clock ticking toward the next transition. In these spaces, you're not just lifting or running; you're practicing for the rhythm of a race. The equipment is selected to support a highly repetitive, high-efficiency format, which means you can push through full circuits without hunting for pieces of gear or waiting for a free lane. There's a sense of momentum that comes from moving from one station to the next with precision and purpose. The atmosphere often promotes accountability, as workouts are typically time-based and team-oriented: you feed off the focus of others, and that shared energy can push you to hit a pace you might not sustain on your own.

Regular gyms, by contrast, are vast ecosystems with a different kind of flexibility. You may find free weights, squat racks, machines, treadmills, a few battle ropes, maybe a squat rack with a bench and an assortment of kettlebells. The variety is valuable because it lets you chase broad health goals—muscle-building blocks, mobility, recovery work, and a steady cadence of longer aerobic sessions. Yet the very breadth of a regular gym can make a HYROX template feel scattered at first. There's more decision fatigue, more scheduling friction, and more dependency on your personal discipline to maintain a plan without the cue of a class or a coach.

The key distinction isn't only what's available; it's how you show up to train. In a HYROX gym, the programming almost always arrives tailor-made for the race: a blend of intervals, station work, and tempo efforts that map directly onto the event format. In a traditional gym, you're more likely to craft your own plan, or follow a generic program, which can be perfectly adequate for general fitness but may require more thinking to align with HYROX pacing. The HYROX space is built for consistency and repetition, with clear progression embedded in the structure. A non-HYROX gym rewards variety and self-management, which is excellent for sustainability but risks drift if you don't have a solid plan aligned to HYROX goals.

That said, you don't have to choose one over the other. The strongest HYROX athletes often learn to borrow the best of both worlds. Use a HYROX gym to practice the intricacies of station transitions, high-rep fatigue, and the mental switch from "steady run" to "station-focused grind." Then supplement with a regular gym block to build pure strength, mobility, and tissue resilience that keeps you durable through long cycles of training. The synergy is what unlocks consistent progress rather than a single-season push. If you're short on time or access, you can tailor hybrid days that combine the clock-driven intensity of a HYROX circuit with the freedom to spend a few extra minutes on grip work or posterior-chain development.

Equipment availability isn't the only variable. The social fabric matters just as much. HYROX gyms often cultivate a tight-knit community with regular events, scorekeeping, and early-riser heroics that make coming back feel like a commitment you don't want to break. Regular gyms excel at inclusivity and flexibility, which can be equally motivating when a busy workweek tempts you to skip workouts. The decision, then, becomes a matter of where you train most consistently and what you crave emotionally as you commit to HYROX. When you understand the strengths of each environment, you can arrange training blocks to honor both your body and your calendar.

Practical takeaway: map an anchor period in your calendar—say, a 6- to 8-week HYROX block—then overlay it with a longer 8- to 12-week maintenance plan in a regular gym for strength and mobility. Your best results will come from routines that align with your life as much as with your ambitions. In the end, HYROX is less about where you train and more about how you train with intention, consistency, and a willingness to adapt.

WHEN TO WORK WITH A COACH: THE VALUE OF GUIDANCE

Coaching becomes especially valuable when HYROX stakes are high—whether you're chasing a personal best, returning from an injury, or juggling a busy schedule that makes self-coaching unreliable. A coach brings clarity to a plan that can feel overwhelming in the first weeks. They help you translate a race format into weekly actions and remind you that progress isn't always about chasing the hardest session; it's about showing up consistently and hitting the right stimulus at the right time. A good HYROX coach also acts as a shield against burnout, because they help you curb the urge to chase intensity every day and instead guide you toward smart, sustainable progression.

The right coach doesn't just hand you a set of workouts; they build a relationship with you and your life. They learn your schedule, your strengths and weaknesses, and your non-training responsibilities. They ask about sleep, stress, nutrition, and family commitments, then fit those realities into a plan you can actually follow. They can help you identify whether you should emphasize running volume, station technique, or heavy lifts first, depending on where you stand on the day you begin their program. They also become your objective mirror—spotting compensations, movement inefficiencies, and early signs of fatigue that you might overlook in the daily grind.

Choosing a good coach begins with a conversation that feels more like a collaboration than a shopping trip for workouts. Look for experience with HYROX-specific movements and knowledge of how the race demands integrate with running and lifting. Ask about their track record with clients who share a similar starting point to yours. How many have achieved their PRs, or simply finished their first HYROX, under their guidance? It's important to hear about the coach's philosophy on progression, recovery, and testing. Do they emphasize data or intuition? Do they design block periods with clear entry and exit points so you can see progress and anticipate deloads? The best coaches also value communication. They respond promptly, translate technical terms into actionable cues, and are honest about whether your current plan suits your life, or whether you need adjustments.

A practical way to approach hiring is to start with a short trial period. A few weeks of close coaching can reveal whether their cues resonate with you, whether you respond to their pacing, and whether their feedback is something you can consistently apply. From there, you can decide whether to extend the partnership. Some athletes thrive with weekly check-ins and planned deloads; others prefer a lighter touch with monthly progress reviews. Either way, the purpose is to create a plan you can actually execute, not a fantasy schedule you'll abandon after a few days.

Ultimately, a HYROX coach adds a layer of accountability and personalization that accelerates progress and reduces the mental load of training. They are not magic; they are a collaborator who helps you translate your goals into a sustainable, repeatable routine. If you're serious about seeing real gains, especially if you're balancing work, family, and other passions, a well-chosen coach can be the difference between chasing a goal and achieving it.

DESIGNING HYROX-INSPIRED CLASSES THAT ARE INCLUSIVE AND FUN

Group classes are the bridge between personal training and lifelong adherence. They create community, accountability, and a rhythm that helps athletes show up even on days when motivation is low. A HYROX-inspired class is not a clone of the race; it is a microcosm of its pacing, intensity, and movement vocabulary, scaled to fit the abilities and equipment of your gym. The goal is to mimic the interval nature and station-to-station mindset without overwhelming participants with a perfect replication of the competition. When done well, these classes teach technique, build aerobic capacity, reinforce grip and core endurance, and leave everyone with a sense of accomplishment.

A well-structured HYROX-inspired class begins with a brief, dynamic warm-up that primes the body for both running and high-repetition stations. Mobilization flows target the hips, ankles, shoulders, and thoracic spine because those areas are repeatedly taxed in HYROX-style work. The warm-up should also set the narrative for the class—this is about continuous movement, efficient transitions, and finishing strong rather than chasing maximal loads in every station.

The main block revolves around a circuit that captures the station-to-station rhythm of HYROX. You might set up eight stations, each with a distinct movement pattern—sled push or pull, farmer's carry, a wall ball or thruster challenge, a worm or medicine-ball variation, box jumps or step-ups, a rowing or assault bike tempo piece, tug-of-war style grip work, and a low back and core stability piece. The class would rotate through these stations with short work periods and strict transition times, followed by a brief rest or a water break. The exact configuration is less important than the flow: clear cues, consistent pacing, and predictable rest.

Scaling options keep the class accessible. For beginners, stations might use lighter implements, shorter distances, or reduced reps. For intermediate and advanced athletes, you can increase load, extend the duration of work, or insert higher-intensity transitions that demand sharper technique and faster decision-making. Partners can add a layer of social accountability, with one person maintaining tempo while the other holds a challenging but safe position in a station, then swapping.

The closing segment should emphasize mobility and recovery, with a short cool-down that targets the same hinge points and alignment cues central to the work. Coaches should end with a brief reflection: what did we learn about our pacing, our form, and our willingness to push through discomfort? The aim is not to burn athletes out but to teach them to maintain effort across multiple stations while staying technically sound and mentally focused.

HYROX-inspired group classes are, at their core, laboratories for movement and rhythm. They offer a flexible structure that scales to different levels while preserving the core demands of HYROX: run, push, carry, and recover—repeatedly, efficiently, and with purpose. When well-executed, they build a community around a shared challenge and give participants a concrete, enjoyable path toward mastering the HYROX format in everyday life.

BLENDING HYROX WITH OTHER RACES: A SMARTER APPROACH TO CALENDAR PLANNING

Integrating HYROX into an existing race calendar is less about squeezing more workouts than about weaving HYROX's distinctive demands into a coherent training strategy. The first step is to identify your anchor race. The anchor acts as the central commitment around which everything else orbits. For some athletes, that anchor is a HYROX race itself; for others, it's a marathon, an OCR, or a triathlon. Either approach works, as long as the plan respects the primary energy systems and the rhythms of your events.

When HYROX is the anchor, you have a straightforward path: dedicate blocks for station technique, run conditioning, and high-repetition strength near race windows, then back off to maintain. If your main focus is a multi-sport schedule, HYROX fits in as a high-intensity, performance-enhancing interlude. You'll want to place HYROX blocks during phases of the season where your running and cycling volumes are manageable. The idea is to avoid stacking peak HYROX fatigue on top of peak endurance workloads. Instead, you'll aim for complementary stimulus: run days that improve pace and form, with HYROX days that sharpen station transitions and muscular endurance.

Periodization becomes your guiding principle. In a typical year, you might structure three primary cycles: base, build, and peak. During the base, HYROX sessions help you build functional capacity with moderate intensity while you gradually accumulate running volume. In the build phase, you'll selectively intensify HYROX blocks—short, sharp intervals with shorter rest, designed to heighten tolerance to fatigue without eroding your long runs. The peak phase concentrates on race-specific pacing and execution, with fewer new movements and more practice of the rhythm you'll carry on competition day. In any cycle, recovery remains non-negotiable; adding HYROX load without time for tissues to adapt only invites injury and burnout.

Cross-training with other disciplines requires thoughtful scheduling. If you're training for a triathlon, for example, consider HYROX blocks as a bridge between cycling and running. The endurance base built in cycling transfers well to HYROX's running demands, while the upper-body endurance from station work translates to what you'll need on the swimming and running transitions. OCR athletes can leverage HYROX to improve grip, shoulder stability, and general work capacity, then substitute a season's event-specific runs to suit the terrain and course format. The key is to harmonize intensities and avoid overloading the same system on consecutive days.

Beyond the physical aspect, plan for race-day logistics. HYROX demands steady pacing and precise transitions, whereas other races may penalize a misread tempo more severely. Your plan should reflect these nuances: maintain consistent energy output in HYROX blocks while preserving full-energy readiness for longer runs or technical obstacles in another event. The payoff is a more resilient athlete who can adapt to varied race environments without sacrificing performance across the board.

In practice, that means clear communication with your coach or training partner about calendars, travel, and recovery. It means written weekly plans that translate into daily actions and a commitment to adjust based on how your body feels. It also means embracing hyphenated training—short, focused HYROX days interspersed with longer, steadier endurance sessions—so you finish the season not depleted but stronger and more versatile than ever.

KEEPING TRAINING IN BALANCE: WORK, FAMILY, AND LIFE OUTSIDE THE GYM

HYROX training doesn't happen in a vacuum. It happens in the middle of commitments, deadlines, school runs, late shifts, and weekend plans. The most sustainable athletes are the ones who design training around life rather than trying to squeeze life into training. The first principle is clarity: know what truly matters to you, and protect that space. If your priority is family time on Saturday mornings, then your long run will happen after a school drop-off, not before. If work deadlines loom, you'll carve shorter, more intense sessions the rest of the week and program a lighter day when meetings spike.

The second principle is consistency over perfection. Small, repeatable actions—three days a week of HYROX-style sessions and two lighter mobility days—beat heroic but inconsistent efforts. Consistency creates momentum, and momentum reduces the mental friction that can derail a program. The goal is to create a rhythm you can sustain, even when life throws curveballs.

Communication is your most powerful tool. Share your training calendar with your partner, your kids, or your support network. Translate your workouts into family-friendly language. Instead of saying you'll be at the gym for two hours to lift heavy, frame it as "a focused forty-minute session that will boost my energy for our weekend hike." When others understand the intent behind your training, they're more likely to support it rather than resent it.

Practical scheduling tips are often small but impactful. Prepare some workouts in advance that require minimal setup—an interval-style run on the treadmill, a quick set of station circuits using only dumbbells and a medicine ball, or a mobility flow you can do in a corner of the living room. Make a "bank of workouts" you can choose from when time is tight. Keep your places of training consistent: the same gym, the same time, the same warm-up flow. Habit becomes the engine of progress.

Mindset matters as well. Recognize that there will be days when energy is low. In those moments, reduce the volume, cut the intensity, and focus on technique and form rather than chasing a PR. Recovery deserves as much attention as the workouts themselves. Sleep, hydration, and nutrition are not auxiliary; they are the infrastructure that makes every session possible. A balanced approach isn't a luxury; it's a strategy for longevity in HYROX and in life.

Finally, plan for flexibility rather than rigidity. If a family event runs long, adjust the following day's plan rather than skipping sessions entirely. If work travels disrupt your routine, adapt with a mobile warm-up and a quick interval session in a hotel gym. The capability to adapt without losing the thread is what separates athletes who finish their first HYROX from those who make HYROX a recurring, meaningful part of their lives.

COACHING CLIENTS FOR HYROX: A PRACTICAL FRAMEWORK FOR TRAINERS

For coaches guiding clients through HYROX prep, the work begins with a careful assessment. You're looking for movement quality, neuromuscular efficiency, and the ability to tolerate repeated, high-intensity efforts. Start with a movement screen that highlights hip hinge, knee tracking, ankle dorsiflexion, and shoulder stability. Add running form observations at a comfortable pace and a few short, controlled attempts at the core HYROX movements to gauge technique under fatigue. This initial picture helps you tailor the program and set realistic expectations.

Programming for HYROX should respect the balance between running and station work. You'll want to cap overall weekly load so joints stay healthy while you build a robust work capacity. Your plan will likely weave together running intervals with station practice, ensuring every component receives appropriate emphasis without crushing the other. Structure your weeks to alternate high-intensity station blocks with running-focused sessions and mobility work. The trick is to create density —lots of work in a compact timeframe—without overloading the same tissue.

Progression is the backbone of your client's journey. Start with a foundation of technique, then gradually increase volume, intensity, and complexity. A simple progression could look like a steady rise in station reps and a slight uptick in running tempo every few weeks, followed by a deload week to allow adaptation. As fatigue accumulates, integrate targeted recovery strategies: soft-tissue work, mobility sequences, and emphasis on sleep and nutrition. The client who makes consistent improvements is the one who can trust the process, not the person chasing a weekly peak.

Assessments along the way should be objective and repeated. Time trials, station completion times, and distance covered during a fixed interval can provide tangible feedback that helps both you and your client stay accountable. You'll also want to monitor subjective markers: perceived exertion, confidence in technique, and ease of execution during transitions. These qualitative cues often reveal early signs of fatigue that a stopwatch cannot detect.

A well-structured HYROX plan anticipates real-life constraints. You'll encounter travel days, family obligations, and sudden schedule shifts. Your job is to offer practical alternatives that preserve the training effect. A travel-friendly coach might provide a two- or three-move routine that requires minimal equipment and can be done in a hotel gym or a living room floor. A comprehensive plan includes communication channels for updates, modification requests, and progress reports that keep the client engaged and optimistic about their trajectory.

In the end, coaching HYROX well is about translating a multi-modal race into an executable, sustainable plan that respects the client's life while pushing them to grow. It's a partnership built on trust, method, and the shared belief that a challenging, purposeful journey can blend seamlessly with a full and busy life.

HYROX AS A CATALYST FOR LIFELONG FITNESS

WHAT YOU'VE LEARNED

You came seeking a clear map of HYROX, and you found more than a route to a finish line. You found a framework that scales with you, a way to think about fitness that bridges runs, lifts, and grit in a single, odder-but-more-alive pursuit. The HYROX race format is not just a series of tasks to complete; it is a living training philosophy. It teaches you how endurance and strength can share the same space, how a mile can be trained with heavy carries and how a hard kilometer can reveal gaps in mobility and recovery. In this book you learned to read a race like a story—starting with understanding the rhythm, then aligning your training to the plot twists of fatigue, form, and strategy. The fundamentals you absorbed are not only about HYROX; they're a gateway to smarter, more resilient training in any arena you choose to enter.

WHAT YOU'VE LEARNED

As you moved from concept to concrete plans, you learned to evaluate your starting point honestly. You discovered the power of scalable volume: how to add or subtract load, how to adjust reps per set, and how to shift emphasis from sheer volume to meaningful quality of effort. You practiced building a weekly cadence that balances running, station work, mobility, and rest, all without burning out. The way you learned to sequence workouts—base, build, peak—became a blueprint for almost any goal, not just a HYROX finish. You realized that consistency compounds more reliably than bursts of heroic effort. The real skill is showing up day after day and making the right small choices when life interrupts the training calendar.

WHAT YOU'VE LEARNED

Technique mattered more than bravado. You learned to scale movements in the stations by choosing weights, ranges of motion, or repetitions that kept you moving efficiently rather than grinding to a standstill. You learned to protect your shoulders during carries, to manage core tension during presses, and to synchronize breathing with movement so you could stay calm when the clock punishes you with fatigue. You also learned the quiet art of recovery—sleep, nutrition, and deliberate mobility—not as afterthoughts but as non-negotiable parts of your plan. The book walked you through mental strategies that keep nerves steady and focus sharp, even as the final rounds loom large. The mental game is not a separate skill; it is the tempo that allows physical skill to flourish.

WHAT YOU'VE LEARNED

Finally, you embraced HYROX not as a one-off challenge but as a lens on your life. The discipline you cultivate in training leaks into daily routines: meals become a little more deliberate, work hours a touch more structured, and your posture a touch more upright when you sit or stand. You saw how progress can hide in plain sight—small gains in air hunger, small improvements in grip endurance, small rearrangements of weekly plans that create more energy for the things you care about. The interlocking threads—goal setting, adaptation, recovery, and community—tie every session to a bigger purpose. When you understand that purpose, the number on a finish clock loses its weight, and the journey itself becomes the reward.

WHAT YOU'VE LEARNED

This closing synthesis confirms a core truth: HYROX's value isn't merely competitive thrill; it is a practical springboard for lifelong fitness. The race structure, when trained thoughtfully, teaches you how to show up for yourself across seasons, across life changes, and across days when motivation dips. You now have a toolkit that can be carried into other challenges—another race, a new sport, or just the daily tempo of an active life. The habits you've started are transferable: the habit of preparation, the habit of pacing, the habit of listening to your body and adjusting course. You've learned to expect effort, to respect process, and to trust the process enough to keep showing up. That—including all the feedback you've gained from your body, your schedule, and your goals—is the true takeaway of this journey.

www.ingramcontent.com/pod-product-compliance
Lightning Source LLC
Chambersburg PA
CBHW071243070526
44583CB00017B/2311